YORK NO

General Editors: Profess
of Stirling) & Professor S
University of Beirut)

William Shakespeare

HENRY IV PART 2

Notes by Michael Jardine

BA MA (NEWCASTLE-UPON-TYNE)
PH D (SHAKESPEARE INSTITUTE, BIRMINGHAM)
Lecturer in English Literature,
King Alfred's College, Winchester

 LONGMAN
YORK PRESS

The illustrations of The Globe Playhouse are from
The Globe Restored in Theatre: A Way of Seeing by
Walter C. Hodges, published by Oxford University
Press. © Oxford University Press

YORK PRESS
Immeuble Esseily, Place Riad Solh, Beirut.

LONGMAN GROUP UK LIMITED
Longman House, Burnt Mill, Harlow,
Essex CM20 2JE, England
Associated companies, branches and representatives
throughout the world

© Librairie du Liban 1981

First published 1981
Second impression 1991

ISBN 0-582-78167-1

Produced by Longman Group (FE) Ltd.
Printed in Hong Kong

Contents

Part 1: Introduction   *page* 5

  The life of William Shakespeare (1564–1616)   5

  The theatre in Shakespeare's time   6

  Historical background   9

  The reign of Henry IV   10

  The Elizabethan attitude to history   11

  Shakespeare's use of English history   12

  The Elizabethan world picture   13

  The literary background   14

  A note on the text   15

Part 2: Summaries   17

  A general summary   17

  Detailed summaries   18

Part 3: Commentary   40

  Date and sources   40

  The relationship between the two parts of *Henry IV*   41

  The nature of the play   42

  The structure of the play   43

  Age and disease: Imagery in the play   44

  Law and order and individual freedom   46

  Falstaff and his rejection   48

  Prince Henry   49

  King Henry IV   51

  The other characters   52

  The language of the play   57

4 · Contents

Part 4: Hints for study   60
  Writing an essay   63
  Specimen essay   64
  Essay questions   67

Part 5: Suggestions for further reading   68

The author of these notes   72

Part 1

Introduction

The life of William Shakespeare (1564–1616)

Shakespeare was born in Stratford-upon-Avon in 1564 and died in the same small market-town fifty-two years later, having spent about half his life in London. Although he never attended university, we can assume that he received a good education at the local grammar school, as his father at this time was a prosperous citizen, who held various civic offices. At such a school Shakespeare would have received a good grounding in the classics, rhetoric, logic and some modern literature.

In 1582 he married Anne Hathaway, who was eight years his senior. A daughter, Susanna, was born in 1583 and twins, Judith and Hamnet (who died eleven years later) in 1585. We can only conjecture about his life during the next seven years. At some point he decided to leave his family, perhaps joining one of the troupes of actors, based in London, who toured the country, since we next hear of him as an established actor and playwright in London. By 1592 he had already made sufficient impact to cause a rival playwright, Robert Greene, to make the following attack on him: 'there is an upstart Crow, beautified with our feathers, that . . . is in his owne conceit the onely Shake-scene in a countrey.' However, in response to this, a writer named Henry Chettle refers to Shakespeare's 'vprightness of dealing, and his facetious grace in writting.'

Despite the opposition of the puritanical magistrates, theatres were thriving in London at this time, acting companies having established themselves in permanent, specially built theatres outside the jurisdiction of the magistrates. The various companies were protected by the patronage of a number of powerful nobles. In 1594 a new company was formed under the patronage of the Lord Chamberlain and Shakespeare was one of eight men who put up money for the venture. As a writer, investor (or 'sharer of the profits'), as well as an actor for some time, he was heavily involved in this company, and the unequalled popularity of his own plays brought both him and the company – the Chamberlain's Men – prosperity. In 1597 he bought the second largest house in Stratford, and by now his family, having purchased a coat of arms, could be styled gentlemen.

Shakespeare's thirty-seven plays (a quarter of which are history plays) were written over a period of some twenty-four years from about 1588 to

1612, at about which time he retired to Stratford. His greatness was recognised by his contemporaries. More of his plays were published and presented at court than any other playwright's, and as early as 1598 one Francis Meres considered, 'Shakespeare among the English is the most excellent in both kinds [tragedy and comedy] for the stage.'

'He was not of an age, but for all time.' This line from Ben Jonson's (1572–1637) memorial poem, written by this famous playwright and poet to preface Shakespeare's collected plays in 1623, anticipated a degree of universality and popularity unparalleled by any other writer the world has seen.

Knowledge of his life and times can help to explain the breadth of his appeal. He was familiar with all aspects of life in both city and country; he was from the middle ranks of society, but mixed with those below, who frequented the theatre, and those above, with whom he had contact both in the theatre and at court (he is known to have enjoyed the patronage of the Earl of Southampton, to whom he dedicated two narrative poems). His lack of a university education may also be relevant in this respect, as his own reading appears to have ranged over a broad spectrum of subjects not covered by universities at that time. He was also fortunate in the timing of his arrival in the dramatic world of London, as he was able to make use of developments in verse writing and dramaturgy made by such playwrights as Thomas Kyd (1558?–94?) or John Lyly (1554?–1606).

The theatre in Shakespeare's time

In trying to understand the way in which a play by Shakespeare works it is helpful to know the kind of playhouse, stage and audience for which it was designed. The first permanent, specially built playhouse, The Theatre, was constructed in 1575–6. Before this, plays were acted in private houses, public halls, market-places, bear-baiting houses and, above all, in the courtyards of inns. The players expected the audience to encircle, or almost encircle them, hence the acting area in the early playhouses jutted out into an uncovered circle of ground, where the poorest members of the audience, the 'groundlings', stood. Shakespeare wrote most of his plays for the Globe Theatre (built in 1599), which had a stage twenty-seven and a half feet deep and forty-three feet wide, and could hold two to three thousand people. Those who could afford not to have to stand with the ill-reputed groundlings sat under cover in circular, tiered galleries, which were interrupted by the 'tiring-house' behind the stage, in which the actors changed (and which contained a 'balcony' which could be used in the play).

There were a number of other companies using different playhouses, so Shakespeare could not afford to miscalculate public taste or he would lose his audience to these rivals or to the bear-baiting pits, which were in the same locality. The rival companies copied, and were even known to steal each others' successful plays. It may well be the case that Shakespeare's plays involving Prince Hal (Henry V) were designed to compete with a play called *The Famous Victories of Henry the Fifth*, performed by the main rival company, the Admiral's Men.

The same plays which were performed on the public stage were sometimes requested at the royal court or in great lords' houses for a private showing. Shakespeare's company acted *Henry IV* privately before the Flemish ambassador in 1600, so we can see that it is a play

THE GLOBE PLAYHOUSE

The theatre, originally built by James Burbage in 1576, was made of wood (Burbage had been trained as a carpenter). It was situated to the north of the River Thames on Shoreditch in Finsbury Fields. There was trouble with the lease of the land, and so the theatre was dismantled in 1598, and reconstructed 'in an other forme' on the south side of the Thames as the Globe. Its sign is thought to have been a figure of the Greek hero Hercules carrying the globe. It was built in six months, its galleries being roofed with thatch. This caught fire in 1613 when some smouldering wadding, from a cannon used in a performance of Shakespeare's *Henry VIII*, lodged in it. The theatre was burnt down, and when it was rebuilt again on the old foundations, the galleries were roofed with tiles.

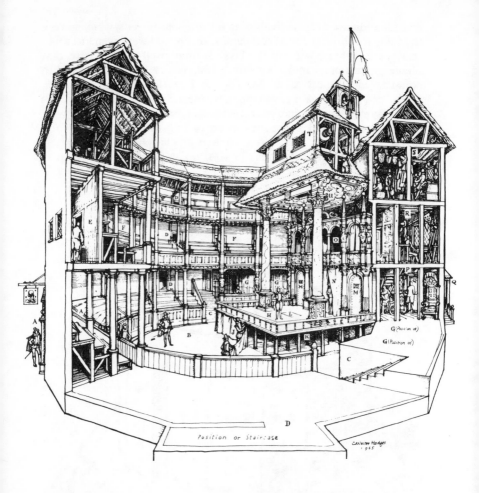

A CONJECTURAL RECONSTRUCTION OF THE INTERIOR OF THE GLOBE PLAYHOUSE

AA Main entrance
 B The Yard
CC Entrances to lowest gallery
 D Entrance to staircase and upper galleries
 E Corridor serving the different sections of the middle gallery
 F Middle gallery ('Twopenny Rooms')
 G 'Gentlemen's Rooms' or 'Lords' Rooms'
 H The stage
 J The hanging being put up round the stage
 K The 'Hell' under the stage
 L The stage trap, leading down to the Hell
MM Stage doors

N Curtained 'place behind the stage'
O Gallery above the stage, used as required sometimes by musicians, sometimes by spectators, and often as part of the play
P Back-stage area (the tiring-house)
Q Tiring-house door
R Dressing-rooms
S Wardrobe and storage
T The hut housing the machine for lowering enthroned gods, etc., to the stage
U The 'Heavens'
W Hoisting the playhouse flag

which was capable of satisfying the tastes of the entire range of Elizabethan society. Falstaff, in particular, had a wide appeal, and Queen Elizabeth herself is said to have requested his return after seeing him in *Henry IV*. One attraction which helped to unite this disparate audience was the element of spectacle in Elizabethan theatre. The stage itself was magnificent, lavishly decorated and colourful, and the plays also gave plenty of opportunity for spectacular effects, such as expert sword-fights, dancing, acrobatics, fireworks and processions (the Globe was burnt to the ground after a cannon was fired on the stage in a performance). Stage properties and costumes added to the spectacle. A theatre-manager's list includes a hell-mouth, a frame for beheading, a chariot, a tree of golden apples and a dragon. Immense sums were spent on costumes. Henry V's coronation robes in Act V of *2 Henry IV* would have been a major attraction, and the grand procession would have made a significant contrast with the rejected Falstaff, dressed in old clothes, 'stained with travel, and sweating' (V.5.24).

In his Prologue to *Henry V*, the sequel to *2 Henry IV*, Shakespeare apologises for the limitations of his stage: 'Piece out our imperfections with your thoughts,' he asks the audience, in order to imagine two vast armies engaged in battle on the stage. As he lacked modern lighting techniques and mechanical aids, or a curtain to bring down while sets could be changed, Shakespeare depended more on language to establish location and to stimulate an imaginative response. In *2 Henry IV* he avoids the problems of *Henry V* by having no fighting at all, except for a tavern brawl between Falstaff and Pistol. Whereas *1 Henry IV* shows us military honour, in *2 Henry IV* we have to imagine it through the brilliant description of Hotspur given by his widow (II.3.18ff.). It is fitting for this rather sombre play that spectacular theatrical effects should be, for the most part, avoided.

Historical background

When Shakespeare came to write his two plays on the reign of Henry IV near the end of the sixteenth century, England was apparently enjoying a period of peace and stability after some forty years under the reign of one monarch, Elizabeth I (1558–1603). The stability depended very much, however, on the ability of Elizabeth to control the numerous discordant elements in the country. At her court there were opposing factions of strong nobles, who, like Northumberland or the Archbishop of York in *2 Henry IV*, wished for greater power and influence. Other discontented groups were dissatisfied with the Established Church, which had broken away from Roman Catholicism during the reign of Elizabeth's father, Henry VIII. Some, such as the Puritans, wished to move further from Rome, while others still had Catholic sympathies. A third source of conflict was the reluctance of Parliament to finance a government over which it had no control.

Within forty years of Elizabeth's death England was convulsed by a terrible civil war. Puritanism and Parliamentarianism combined to overthrow a king whose court was weakened by factions. Charles I, the son of Elizabeth's successor, tried to govern without Parliament (a mistake which Henry V was keen to avoid; see *2 Henry IV*, V.2.134 and V.5.106) and was executed in 1649. We must wonder, then, whether a belief in the sanctity of kingship was unquestioningly held by thinking people even during Elizabeth's reign. It seems clear that by the time Shakespeare wrote *2 Henry IV* her popularity was beginning to wane. Years of famine and inflation, grave concern about the ageing queen's refusal to name a successor and the private grievances of some ambitious courtiers (leading to the Essex rebellion in 1601) had undermined the popularity which had been at its height after the defeat of a Spanish invasion fleet (the Armada) in 1588.

Although there was peace at home, from 1585 until 1603 England was continually at war either in the Netherlands or Ireland or on the high seas, and soldiers must have been a common sight in Shakespeare's London:

What! A young knave, and begging! Is there not wars?

(*2 Henry IV*, I.2.72–3)

Falstaff's question had contemporary relevance. So had Henry IV's advice to 'busy giddy minds. With foreign quarrels' (*2 Henry IV*, IV.5.213–14) as Elizabeth seems to have tried to do just that, and recruiting officers like Falstaff would not have been an uncommon sight. Although set two hundred years in the past, *2 Henry IV* reveals much about social conditions in Elizabethan England, for instance, the widening gap between rich and poor as a result of inflation, over-population in London and unemployment. As Henry IV observes,

Fortune . . . either gives a stomach and no food –
Such are the poor, in health – or else a feast
And takes away the stomach – such are the rich.

(*2 Henry IV*, IV.4.103–7)

The reign of Henry IV

Henry Bolingbroke, exiled son of the Duke of Lancaster, returned to England in 1399 to claim his inheritance, which the present king, Richard II, had confiscated on Bolingbroke's father's death. He consolidated opposition against Richard, who was eventually forced to abdicate and was murdered in prison in 1400. Bolingbroke was crowned but as a usurper his position was vulnerable. He had no serious claim to succeed Richard, who had, in fact, named Edmund, Earl of March, as his successor in 1398. To claim that Richard's bad government forfeited his right to rule would undermine the sanctity of kingship. If Henry IV relied on Parliament to legalise his succession, this would give powers to a body which could be used against him, and it would also set a dangerous precedent of claiming the throne as a right of conquest.

The very nobles who had helped him to the crown, such as the Earl of Northumberland, felt powerful enough to try to depose him when he dissatisfied them. Two rebellions against him form the central actions of 1 Henry IV and 2 Henry IV. The first, called the Percy Rebellion, ended with a victory for Henry IV at the battle of Shrewsbury (1403), and the second, led by Archbishop Scrope, ended at York, without a battle, in 1405. Scrope was tricked by Westmorland (not Prince John, as Shakespeare has it) into disbanding his army. Northumberland and Bardolph fled to Scotland, but were killed in battle in 1408. Shakespeare's emphasis on instability only really applies to the first half of Henry's reign, but in the second half he was troubled by sickness. His eldest son, Prince Henry, filled the gap left by the king's protracted illness and ill-feeling developed between the prince and his father, who resented his son's ambition for power.

The Elizabethan attitude to history

You may wonder why Shakespeare chose to set so many of his plays either in the past or in foreign countries, if he was concerned with his own times. The simple fact is that government censorship made it difficult to introduce contemporary English figures on to the stage. A royal proclamation of 1559 made it an offence punishable with imprisonment for plays to be performed 'wherein either matters of religion or of the governaunce of estate of the common weale shall be handled or treated'. Shakespeare had to alter the name of his fat knight from Oldcastle to Falstaff, because, it is believed, the noble family of Cobham protested at having their ancestor presented as such a figure. We can tell from this, however, that Elizabethans were more sensitive to their past than we are, and that perhaps using historical subjects would not have appeared limiting to Shakespeare. History was viewed not as the study of a dead past but as the key to a proper understanding of the present. Parallels were easily drawn between past and current events as many Elizabethans believed that history is cyclical.

The tetralogy or sequence of four plays of which 2 Henry IV is the third, written by Shakespeare between 1590 and 1599, deals with what was seen by Elizabethans as a period of English history providing significant parallels with their own situation. It covers the fall of the Plantagenets (in *Richard II*) and the rise of the Lancastrians (in *1 Henry IV, 2 Henry IV* and *Henry V*), who were eventually overthrown by the Tudors, Elizabeth I's ancestors. The single event which overshadows this period of history is the deposition of Richard II, and we should remember that Queen Elizabeth I believed that people drew a parallel between her reign and Richard's. She is recorded as saying: 'I am King Richard, know ye not that'. In 1601, before leading an armed rebellion in London, the Earl of Essex paid Shakespeare's company to perform *Richard II*, (including the deposition scene which had been censored when the play was published in 1597), in order to gain popular support for his rising. We can understand, then, why certain passages of *2 Henry IV* which contain allusions to the overthrow and murder of Richard were excised when the play was first published in 1600.

English history clearly could be used as propaganda on behalf of as well as against a government. In 1600 a historian, Sir John Hayward, who wrote a book on Henry IV, was imprisoned because Elizabeth's ministers believed it to be directed against her government. The 'official' version of the period had been written by historians who were specially commissioned by Tudor monarchs, and hence interpreted history in a way most flattering to them. These histories, called chronicles, established what is known as the Tudor Myth. They presented pre-Tudor history from 1398 to 1485 as a period of unrest and civil disorder (with the exception of Henry V's reign) characterised by weak, troubled or tyrannical monarchs, which gives way to a period of peace, prosperity and order under the Tudors. The political lesson drawn from these past events is that to depose or rebel against your lawful king, as happened to Richard II, is to plunge the country into chaos. Some critics, notably E. M. W. Tillyard,* argue that Shakespeare adopts this formula for his dramatisation of the period, but more recent critics have shown that there were conflicting contemporary interpretations which used this same period to demonstrate the established right of a people to depose a monarch who put himself above the law. Shakespeare is just as likely to have subscribed to the latter interpretation.

Shakespeare's use of English history

Shakespeare wrote ten plays based on English chronicle history, and these form his only consistent attempt at a type of play for which he apparently had no precedent. *King John* and *Henry VIII* apart, these plays seem to aim at a completeness and a continuity over five consecutive reigns from the death of Richard II to the death of Richard III, which, again, is a use of history in drama peculiar to Shakespeare. There is plenty of evidence to suggest that he viewed history as a

*Tillyard, E. M. W., *Shakespeare's History Plays*, Chatto and Windus, London, 1944.

continuous narrative. We are often projected backwards or forwards in time, beyond the limits of each play, and he is careful to build up characters at the end of one play who will be prominent in the next. The ending of 2 *Henry IV* serves also as an introduction to the next play in the sequence, *Henry V*, as we are shown the start of that king's reign and told of his future wars in France and his wooing of the French princess, Katherine.

This element of continuity shows that political acts are not isolated events but have consequences beyond the immediate present. This puts a heavy burden on the men who make political decisions, which may, like Henry IV's deposition of Richard II, haunt them for the rest of their lives, and even harm their children's children. In the history plays Shakespeare is very much concerned with the man behind the role, the nature of the individual king, prince or lord whose choices may affect the life of a nation. The gap between the role or office, the crown which never dies, and the person, who suffers, grows ill and surely dies, creates much of the dramatic effect of the history plays.

Shakespeare may have been using this period of English history to demonstrate God's providence, the working out of a divine plan, involving recurrent civil wars as a punishment for deposing a legitimate king. It could also be argued that when he looked back at medieval England he saw its history as a spectacle of human failure repeating the same mistakes in a 'cruel cycle'* of usurpation, treachery and betrayal, so that history stands still and prophecies can be made with assurance (see *2 Henry IV*, III.1.45–90 and IV.1.195–202).

The Elizabethan world picture

Shakespeare was writing during a period of transition from a rigid medieval feudal society based on rank to a more mobile capitalist society based on commerce, but the medieval world-view was still a powerful influence as it pictured an ordered and harmonious universe at a time of upheaval and doubt. Its attraction lay in its completeness and simplicity, as every element in God's creation is given a fixed place in its hierarchical system. Central to this system is the idea of a Great Chain of Being linking each element, according to its degree of excellence, from God down to inanimate matter. Humans are placed below angels but above animals, and within human kind the king is at the top and the peasant at the bottom of the scale. The ideal human society corresponds to the harmony apparent elsewhere in the universe, just as the well-ordered individual achieves a balance of warring elements (called 'humours') in his body. Disorder only comes in society when the natural

*The idea of a repeated 'cruel cycle' in Shakespeare's presentation of history is developed in Jan Kott, *Shakespeare Our Contemporary*, Methuen, London, 1964, p. 31.

order is upset; sickness or ill-temper only strike the human body when the humours (melancholy, blood, choler, phlegm) are wrongly proportioned (see *2 Henry IV*, IV.4.62–6).

2 Henry IV is full of images of disorder and disease, and, according to the system outlined above, it could be argued that the unhealthy society results from a disturbance in the natural order when Henry IV deposed King Richard II. According to a current theory called the Divine Right of Kings, kings were chosen by God, were above man-made laws, and could not be deposed by their subjects. Thus the rebels in *2 Henry IV* are able to claim they are not bringing disorder, but are merely symptoms of a disorder brought about by Henry IV's usurpation, which, Henry himself admits, casts a shadow over his reign (see IV.5.183–6). The fact that characters in the history plays believe that the troubled nature of Henry's reign is punishment for usurpation does not, however, indicate that the playwright accepted the medieval world-view. The range of political and social ideas presented in *2 Henry IV* is vastly more complex than this. As a man who had raised himself to the rank of gentleman by his success in business, Shakespeare must have had doubts about a world-view according to which it was considered unnatural to try to change one's place in the social hierarchy.

The literary background

Shakespeare's success can be partly accounted for by the period in which he wrote, which was the height of the English Renaissance, an artistic, literary and scientific revival, which originated in Italy in the fourteenth century with the rediscovery of forgotten Latin and Greek texts. In sixteenth-century England Latin authors in particular were widely studied in grammar schools and universities, and the advent of printing presses enabled a wider dissemination of learning. The Renaissance brought with it a dramatic increase in intellectual activity, a wish to experiment, to discover and to compete, as Englishmen, with the best of classical authors and their continental imitators. The publication in 1579 of Edmund Spenser's (1552?–99) poem *The Shepheardes Calender* is often seen as marking the beginning of the golden age of English literature, as here was a work written by an Englishman in his own language which invited and withstood comparison with the best modern European and classical poetry.

Drama benefited from the revival of learning in a number of ways. Members of the nobility, conscious of their responsibilities as patrons, became interested in plays, and their involvement both as sponsors and audience raised the level of theatrical productions. The four or more theatrical companies, who changed their programme regularly, needed a continuous flow of play scripts and these were mostly provided by unemployed university graduates, whose knowledge of Latin plays and classical rhetoric inevitably influenced their writing. This influence can be seen in the adaptation of plots of Latin plays, the adoption of a five act structure, a widespread use of classical allusions and the introduction of stock characters, such as the 'braggart soldier' (whom Pistol resembles and with whom Falstaff has some shared traits). A belief in the need for a knowledge of rhetoric, which gave training in the most effective ways to make speeches, was a great influence on the entire literature of the period, and particularly on Elizabethan drama, which depends so much on the effectiveness of speech. Shakespeare's familiarity with rhetorical 'tricks', particularly puns, figures of speech and repeated verbal patterns, is most apparent in his earliest plays, but is continually evident in the language of *2 Henry IV*; for example in Northumberland's speech:

> these news
> Having been well, that would have made me sick,
> Being sick, have in some measure made me well.

(I.1.137–9)

Although influenced by classical drama and the plays of the university men, Shakespeare's roots can be found in the native dramatic tradition. In his lifetime medieval plays on biblical subjects, called miracle plays, were still being performed, but a greater influence was the so-called morality play. This was a didactic form involving personified abstractions such as Youth, Age and Vice (the relationship between Hal, the Lord Chief Justice and Falstaff may draw on such a morality scheme). In the 1560s and 1570s moralities began to incorporate material from the historical chronicles, and alongside the allegorical abstractions 'real' characters were represented. The moral element of such plays (which are sometimes called interludes) would be enlivened by songs, dances, scurrility and slapstick comedy. Both in themes and in structure (notice the blend of farcical and serious elements in *2 Henry IV*) these interludes had a lasting influence on Shakespeare's plays.

A note on the text

When Shakespeare completed a play he was paid a fee and gave up all rights of ownership. It is not known for certain why some of his plays were published in a printed text during his lifetime. One route from playhouse to printing press was by piracy, a member of the audience or the company providing a stolen version or one reconstructed from memory, which could lead to a better text being published to supersede the pirated one. Other explanations are that plays were sold because of shortage of funds at times when theatres were closed on account of the plague, or that companies sometimes cleared out old plays no longer part of their repertoire.

2 Henry IV is one of nineteen plays by Shakespeare which appeared in a Quarto form published during his lifetime, and not only in the Folio edition of collected plays published in 1623. ('Folio' is twice the size of 'quarto', being a sheet of paper folded once only, and was the format used for prestigious publications.) Unlike *1 Henry IV*, which went through seven editions, the Quarto of *2 Henry IV* appeared in one edition only in 1600. It is probably derived from Shakespeare's 'foul papers' (the draft which preceded his fair copy) and it differs considerably from the Folio text, the source for which is unknown, so that the main task of the modern editor is to provide a text based on preferred readings from these two sources. The Folio version contains 168 lines omitted from the Quarto, which had probably been censored as they concern the deposition of Richard II. The censor did not see the longer references to Richard in Act III Scene 1 because this scene had been mislaid in the printing-house. We know this because the Quarto exists in two states, one of which includes the missing scene which the printer inserted half way through the issue.

Some traces of the name of Oldcastle, the name originally given to Falstaff (changed under pressure from Oldcastle's descendants), remain in the speech-prefixes in the early part of *2 Henry IV*. This indicates that Shakespeare must have started writing it before *1 Henry IV* was entered in the Stationers' Register on 25 February 1598, as the alterations from Oldcastle to Falstaff had been made in this play. It is likely that *2 Henry IV* was not much more than begun by this date as the title page of the earlier play omits the words 'First Part'. The two versions of the epilogue in *2 Henry IV*, the later of which contains an apology about Oldcastle, suggest that the play was completed before protests were made, between 1597 and 1598, about the use of that name, and that Shakespeare felt the need to make amends for the slur on Oldcastle at some time before starting *Henry V* in the spring of 1599.

As different modern editions have different line numbers it is necessary to use one particular edition throughout this commentary. The one selected is the easily available edition in the New Penguin Shakespeare series:

WILLIAM SHAKESPEARE, *Henry IV, Part 2*, edited by P. Davison, Penguin Books, Harmondsworth, 1977.

Part 2

Summaries
of HENRY IV PART 2

A general summary

The Earl of Northumberland, who is awaiting news of his son's rebellion against King Henry IV, at first receives false information but then learns that his son's army has been defeated at the battle of Shrewsbury and he himself has been killed. Stirred to action by this news the earl plans to unite with another group of rebellious nobles led by the Archbishop of York. In London Mistress Quickly arranges to have Falstaff arrested for debt, but Falstaff manages to persuade her against this course of action, and even borrows more money from her. Prince Henry and his friend Poins plan to disguise themselves as barmen and spy on Falstaff as he entertains Doll Tearsheet, a woman of ill repute, and other friends. In high spirits after having driven off the swaggering Pistol, Falstaff insults Prince Henry and Poins, who emerge from their disguise to challenge him.

News from the court of preparations to oppose the rebel army leads to Prince Henry's hurried departure. Meanwhile the king is bowed by the troubles of his unquiet reign and is filled with guilt for having seized the crown from Richard II, the legitimate king. Falstaff, now recruiting for the king's army, arrives at Justice Shallow's house where he conscripts the three men who do not pay him a bribe. Northumberland's earlier passion for revenge has now diminished and he plans to flee to Scotland. The other rebel leaders, weakened by Northumberland's absence, agree terms of peace with Prince John, but as soon as their army has dispersed Prince John orders their arrest and sends them to be executed.

The news of this victory fails to comfort the ailing king. He is carried to his bed where he lies apparently dead, and Prince Henry takes the crown from his bedside, thinking it now to be his. The king, however, recovers and accuses his son of wishing him dead. Prince Henry manages to appease his father, and the king in a final speech before his death advises him how best to govern England.

Henry V's accession is awaited fearfully by the court and by the Lord Chief Justice in particular, because the prince has a reputation for riotous conduct. Their fears prove unfounded as the new king promises to abide by the laws of the land and restores the Lord Chief Justice to his post. Ignorant of this change, Falstaff rushes from Shallow's house and presents himself before the new king expecting favour and reward, but he is spurned and sent to prison with his company.

Detailed summaries

Induction

Rumour introduces himself as a dominant force on earth, with the power to spread false alarm and uncertainty. He announces his present task to be the circulation of news of a victory for Hotspur against the king's forces at Shrewsbury, which is the reverse of the truth. He prepares us for the reception of these 'smooth comforts false' (line 40) by Hotspur's father, the Earl of Northumberland.

Rumour is an appropriate figure to introduce this play, which is characterised by uncertainty, fraud and guile. The Induction establishes the tone of the play and is far from being 'wholly useless' as the famous critic, poet and essayist Dr Johnson (1709–84) asserted.

NOTES AND GLOSSARY:

Induction:	a scene or monologue introducing the main action
painted full of tongues:	(*stage direction*) Rumour was traditionally personified as a figure covered in tongues illustrating its slanderous character
drooping:	refers to sunset
post-horse:	horses available at stages of a journey for carriers of post (or other travellers)
still:	continually
musters:	recruitment of troops, a common occurrence in England at this time when Spanish invasion was feared
And no such matter:	though such fears are unfounded
so plain a stop:	so easily played upon. The 'stops' of a 'pipe' (line 15) or flute are the holes fingered to produce various sounds
the blunt . . . heads:	the general populace, seen as a fickle and insensitive mob (as in I.2.87–108)
wavering:	unsteady, vacillating
anatomize:	analyse, dissect
my household:	the world, which is under his influence; also the theatre audience
King Harry's victory:	at the battle of Shrewsbury, which forms the climax of *1 Henry IV*. Henry could be changed to Harry or Hal
Harry Monmouth:	Prince Hal, who was born at Monmouth
Douglas' rage:	Douglas is a rebel in *1 Henry IV*, driven off by Hal who thus saves the King's life
hold:	castle

| crafty-sick: | feigning sickness (see I.1.145–9) |
| posts . . . on: | couriers riding to exhaustion |

Act I Scene 1

Northumberland, awaiting news from the battle-front, is visited by Lord Bardolph, who announces a rebel victory. Later arrivals, Travers and Morton, the latter giving an eye-witness report, contradict Bardolph and announce defeat and the death of Northumberland's son, Hotspur. The earl is aroused to a 'stormy passion' (line 165) and vows to inflict chaos on Henry IV's England. Morton pacifies him and reminds him of another conspiracy to overthrow King Henry, led by the Archbishop of York, and Northumberland now prepares to temper his revenge with a concern for 'safety' (line 213).

NOTES AND GLOSSARY:

keeps:	guards
attend:	wait
high:	over-rich
an:	if
in the fortune of:	as for what has befallen
both the Blunts:	Shakespeare mentions only Sir Walter Blunt in *1 Henry IV*
Stafford:	the Earl of Stafford, who, like Blunt, was disguised as the king at Shrewsbury and killed by Douglas
brawn:	a boar fattened for eating
hulk:	a large ship, applied to Falstaff because of his obesity
Caesar's fortunes:	Caius Julius Caesar (101–44BC), who conquered Britain and greatly extended the Roman Empire
forspent:	exhausted
breathe:	allow to regain his breath
spur . . . cold:	Hotspur (Harry Percy) being dead is cold
jade:	a worn-out horse
rowel-head:	a small spiked wheel on a spur
Staying:	waiting for
have not the day:	has not won the battle
point:	a piece of lace used to tie up articles of clothing
hilding:	base
at a venture:	recklessly
title-leaf:	the title-page, which at this time described the contents of the book
witnessed usurpation:	the wrinkled effect of the sea visible on a beach ('strand') when the tide is out

Priam: the last King of Troy, killed by the Greeks after their successful siege of the city

found . . . tongue: discovered the fire before the man had the courage to tell him of it

is chanced: has happened

Rendering faint quittance: giving weak resistance

In few: in few words, briefly

Being bruited once: once the news of it had spread

best-tempered: as of metal, the finest mixture

three times . . . the King: to confuse the enemy the king had several noblemen wear the same dress as himself. Three were killed in battle (see *1 Henry IV*, V.4.39–40)

Gan vail his stomach: began to lose his courage

In poison . . . well: Elizabethans believed certain poisons had medicinal value, thus Northumberland considers bad news as having power to cure his present sickness

under life: beneath the weight of the living man

keeper: nurse

nice: unmanly; also delicate

scaly gauntlet: a long glove made of overlapping pieces of metal

coif: nightcap

wanton: effeminate

fleshed: having tasted blood, thirsting for more

ragged'st: roughest

Let order die: words that would shock an Elizabethan audience, as they do Morton, and they make Northumberland at this point appear criminally insane

feed . . . act: foster dispute in a long-drawn-out action (or act of a play)

Cain: in the Bible (Genesis 4) he is the son of Adam and Eve who commits the first murder

rude scene: discordant action (also completing the stagecraft metaphor, 'stage . . . act . . . scene', which allows these remarks to be applied to the dramatist's art as well as to the scene depicted)

cast th'event: estimated the outcome

make head: raise an army

dole: dealing out

forward: eager

trade of danger: interchange of dangerous blows

stiff-borne: obstinately pursued

engagèd to: concerned with

wrought out life: survived

respect: consideration

gentle:	well-born (as in gentleman). The archbishop was related to the Earl of Wiltshire, whose execution by Henry IV is said to have angered him (see *1, Henry IV* I.3.264–5)
double surety:	by bodily and spiritual allegiance
corpse:	the body alone, without the will or soul
to fight:	to fight on his behalf
potions:	draughts of medicine
Turns insurrection to religion:	makes rebellion a holy act; a paradox, as rebellion was commonly considered a crime against God, as kings were God's representatives
enlarge:	enhance
Pomfret:	the murder of Richard II at this castle takes place in Act V Scene 5 of Shakespeare's *Richard II*
Bolingbroke:	another name for Henry IV
more or less:	upper and lower classes of people
posts:	couriers
make:	gather together

Act I Scene 2

Falstaff, proud of his undeserved honours resulting from the battle of Shrewsbury, is seen with his page (a present from his friend Prince Hal) in a London street. He is challenged by the Lord Chief Justice, who wishes to bring charges against him for a robbery he has committed (described in *1 Henry IV*, II.2). He decides not to do so because of Falstaff's reputed heroism (see *1 Henry IV*, V.4.126).

NOTES AND GLOSSARY:

buckler:	shield. The carrying of the sword and buckler emphasises Falstaff's status as a knight, and recalls the false rumour of his heroism at Shrewsbury
giant:	ironical, as the page is very small
water:	urine
owed:	owned
gird:	gibe, jeer
foolish-compounded clay:	compounded of folly, created from clay
intends:	tends, inclines
whoreson mandrake:	abominable midget (mandrake being a plant with a forked root said to resemble a man)
worn . . . cap:	like a brooch (again referring to the page's diminutive size)
manned with an agate:	attended by a person the size of a figure carved in ornate stone worn as a jewel

juvenal:	young man
fledge:	covered with down
stick:	hesitate
a face royal:	primarily a first-class face, but also suggesting a face untouched (by a barber) as a stag-royal may only be hunted by the king, perhaps also the face of the king on a ten-shilling coin (called a royal)
writ:	called himself
grace:	(*i*) a title, such as 'your Grace' (*ii*) a favour
slops:	wide breeches
the glutton:	Dives of the Dives and Lazarus parable, who went to hell while the poor man went to heaven (see the Bible, Luke 16). Falstaff seems strongly aware of the Scriptures, which is ironic, given his immoral behaviour, but deepens his association with the morality tradition (see page 15). The Dives parable is also referred to by Falstaff in *1 Henry IV*, III.3.31 and IV.2.33
his tongue be hotter:	Dives begged Lazarus for water to cool his tongue in hell
Achitophel:	in the Bible (Samuel 2:15–17) he is a treacherous counsellor spurned by King David (as Falstaff will be by King Henry)
yea-forsooth:	a mild oath as used by a servile tradesman (the 'knave')
bear in hand:	encourage with false hopes
stand upon:	insist upon
smoothy-pates:	Puritan tradesmen with short hair against the current fashion
high shoes:	with high heels, appropriate for upstarts, as are the 'bunches of keys', which suggest an influential social position
if a man . . . security:	after a man has completed a deal with them they suddenly demand security
ratsbane:	poison
horn of abundance:	(*i*) cornucopia (*ii*) cuckold's horn (as also in 'lanthorn' = lantern)
Smithfield . . . Paul's . . . stews:	a horse market of ill repute; the nave of St Paul's cathedral in London; brothels. Falstaff is referring to a popular saying which advised against these three choices
hunt counter:	make a mistake
his:	its. The normal possessive form of 'it' was 'his': the form 'its' was not in use until about 1600

Galen:	highly regarded Greek physician (*c.* AD 130–*c.* 200); another of Falstaff's numerous learned references
by the heels:	with your legs in fetters or the stocks
make . . . scruple:	have the slightest doubt
land-service:	military service, which would protect Falstaff from a civilian summons
I am . . . my dog:	this has never been explained
exploit on Gad's Hill:	the robbery referred to above (line 60)
quiet o'erposting:	quietly getting away with
smell a fox:	have one's suspicions aroused
wassail candle:	a large candle capable of lasting a whole night, as at a feast. Candles could be made from animal fat (tallow) or beeswax (note the pun on wax = grow)
gravy:	fat from hot meat
ill angel:	each man was believed to be attended by a good and a bad spirit. This is another reference which draws attention to Falstaff's similarity to a Vice figure from the old morality drama. Falstaff puns on the word 'angel' meaning a coin worth one-third of £1, bad if 'light' (underweight)
go:	pass for true money, or, simply, walk
these costermonger's times:	a low type of salesman who sold apples (costards) from a barrow, hence the 'times' were base
bearherd:	the man who looked after the bears used for popular entertainment (rivalling the theatres); he was poorly regarded
pregnancy:	quick-wittedness
in the vaward of our youth:	Falstaff's age and his degeneration are continually referred to in this play, but he claims to be in the forefront ('vaward') of youth
caper with me:	challenge me to a dancing contest
marks:	a mark was worth two-thirds of £1
ashes . . . sack:	the Prince did not mourn in the traditional way but celebrated his act; 'sack' is a type of wine
brandish . . . bottle:	refers back to *1 Henry IV*, V.3.55, when Falstaff takes wine into battle in place of a gun
spit white:	this has no clear meaning, but probably means 'spit clean', that is, healthily
crosses:	(*i*) afflictions (*ii*) coins marked with a cross
fillip . . . beetle:	strike me with a battering-ram needing three men to lift it
both . . . curses:	both stages of life have their own curses which anticipate mine

groats:	coins worth fourpence
Ursula:	possibly Mistress Quickly (see II.1.87)
commodity:	something to sell, self-interest

Act I Scene 3

The rebel leaders, the Archbishop of York, Mowbray, Hastings and Lord Bardolph, meet to discuss their prospects of success in battle against the king's forces. They debate whether or not the presence of Northumberland's assistance is essential. Their approach is cautious and concerned with self-preservation rather than a passionate sense of grievance. The archbishop bases his hopes on the size of their army and the fickle nature of the masses, now tired of the king they preferred to Richard II.

NOTES AND GLOSSARY:

supplies:	reinforcements
marry:	by the Virgin Mary (a mild oath)
project:	anticipation
Yes ... or else:	these twenty lines are omitted from the First Quarto, perhaps because they make little sense
Yes ... th'appearing buds:	possibly 'Yes, *if* the present occasion for war *does* so live in hope, like those we form in spring when buds appear'
When we ... tyranny:	refers to the parable of the builder (see the Bible, Luke 14:28–30) warning against commencing an operation without the resources to complete it
his opposite:	all that stands against the success of the plan
trimmed:	dressed
eat thy dead vomit up:	refers to the multitude and is based on the Bible, Proverbs 26:11 and 2 Peter 2:22

Act II Scene 1

Mistress Quickly has hired officers to arrest Falstaff for debt. The fat knight resists arrest but is scolded by the Lord Chief Justice for unseemly conduct and time-wasting, as he should be making for York to fight the rebels. While Falstaff placates Mistress Quickly (and borrows more money) Gower enters with news of preparations for war and the return to London of the king.

NOTES AND GLOSSARY:

entered the action:	filed the lawsuit
foin:	thrust. Like many of the verbs in this scene there is a hidden sexual meaning

infinitive:	infinite. Mistress Quickly continually invents and misuses words in her effort to sound impressive
score:	account at the tavern
continuantly:	immediately; a blend of 'continually' and 'incontinently'

Pie Corner – saving your manhoods: a part of London once noted for cook-shops, but apparently having more unseemly associations, as the Hostess apologises ('saving' here means 'no offence to')

indited:	for 'invited'
exion:	for 'action'
mark:	the value of two-thirds of £1, not a coin
malmsey-nose:	malmsey is a red wine, the colour of Bardolph's nose

whose mare's dead?: what's the fuss?

quean:	prostitute
channel:	gutter

honeysuckle ... honeyseed: for 'homicidal' and 'homicide'

wot ta:	(*dialect*) wilt thou
rampallian:	ruffian
fustilarian:	possibly formed from the word 'fustilugs', a fat, frowsy woman
catastrophe:	ending
Eastcheap:	an area of London which had associations with butchers' shops and low life
ride ... mare:	haunt your sleep with nightmares
Wheeson:	(*dialect*) Whitsun
liking ... Windsor:	obscure, but possibly meaning 'likening his father to a professional singer' (such as were condemned by Puritans). This particular singer may have been a pretender to the throne, which would explain Hal's annoyance
gossip:	neighbour (a familiar form of address)
green:	fresh
madam:	this title could be claimed when one married a knight
in good case:	well off
sneap:	rebuke
glasses:	Falstaff persuades the Hostess to replace her metal cups with more fashionable glasses

story ... bed-hangers: she should also replace her tapestries with paintings on cloth of comic pictures, hunting scenes or the parable of the prodigal son (see the Bible, Luke 15:11–32)

humours:	moods
nobles:	coins worth one-third of £1
presently:	immediately

Act II Scene 2

Prince Hal and Poins discuss the former's dejected state, which seems to be caused by thoughts of his father's illness and also by the problems he has in coming to terms with his greatness as heir to the crown. Hal receives a pompous letter from Falstaff and plans to spy on the fat knight in disguise.

NOTES AND GLOSSARY:

composition:	refers to the 'small' (that is, weakened) beer, hardly a drink for princes
thy name:	Poins's name, who is his social inferior. But compare 'I know thee not, old man' (V.5.47), Hal's words to Falstaff after his coronation
it is ... racket there:	Poins will be found playing tennis so long as he has a shirt to wear
rest ... holland:	a series of puns: 'rest' as (*i*) repose (*ii*) remainder; 'low countries' as (*i*) Netherlands (*ii*) lower regions of the body (*iii*) brothel areas; 'shift' as (*i*) contrivance (*ii*) shirt; 'holland' as (*i*) country of that name (*ii*) linen. The general meaning is 'Your own low habits have forced you to pawn your shirts'
knows ... kingdom:	knows whether babies dressed in the remnants of your shirts will go to heaven
not in the fault:	not to blame (for being illegitimate)
stand the push:	can stand up to
a second brother:	only the eldest son inherited a family fortune
proper ... hands:	fine fighting fellow
transformed him ape:	dressed him fantastically
get ... maidenhead:	drink a two-quart pot of beer
Althaea's dream:	an image from Greek mythology, but Althaea, wife of the King of Calydon, is here confused with Hecuba, the wife of King Priam of Troy, who dreamed that she would give birth to a firebrand
sixpence to preserve thee:	keep him a Christian, as a 6d. piece bore a cross
martlemas:	a piece of beef fattened for slaughter on Martinmas Day (November 11). This refers to Falstaff's enormous size but also couples him with festivity and the coming of winter (old age)
wen:	tumour, swelling

fetch it from Japhet: trace their ancestry back to Japhet, a son of Noah whose offspring peopled Europe (see the Bible, Genesis 9:27)

certificate: in a formal style

frank: pig-sty (perhaps a reference to a famous tavern called the Boar's Head ('the old place')

Ephesians ... church: libertines (who were chastised by St Paul in his Epistle to the Ephesians 5:18)

Saint Alban's and London: a common route for travellers

drawers: waiters in a bar

Jove's case: Jupiter, the principal Roman god, identified with the Greek god, Zeus, god of the sky. He changed himself into a bull and carried away Europa, daughter of Agenor, a King of Tyre

---

Act II Scene 3

Northumberland's earlier passion for war to avenge his son is cooling and the opposition of his wife and his son's widow to his joining forces with the rebels is sufficient to persuade him to desert their cause and fly to Scotland.

NOTES AND GLOSSARY:

daughter: that is, daughter-in-law

give ... affairs: submit to my harsh course of action

Percy: the earl's family name

glass: mirror, example

speaking thick: Hotspur was an impetuous character who spoke in a hurried manner

affections of delight: tastes for pleasure

humours of blood: moods

nice: punctilious, exact

Monmouth: Prince Hal. As in I.1.109 Hotspur's death is known to have been at the hands of Prince Hal, not Falstaff, who only stabs the dead body (see *1 Henry IV*, V.4.127)

puissance ... taste: power ... trial

rain upon remembrance: cry upon a plant (rosemary) which signifies remembrance

---

Act II Scene 4

Falstaff entertains his friends, including Doll Tearsheet, at an inn. The loud-mouth Pistol interrupts them and is driven off by Falstaff. Hal and

Poins enter in disguise and overhear Falstaff maligning them to Doll. They confront him and Falstaff tries to explain away his insults. News arrives from court that the king is making preparations to attack the rebel army. Prince Hal leaves hurriedly, ashamed of his time-wasting.

NOTES AND GLOSSARY:

apple-johns:	a kind of apple best eaten when old and shrivelled
cover:	lay the table-cloth
old utis:	a grand festival ('utas' or 'utaves' was the eighth day of a feast)
temperality:	temper or temperance
pulsidge:	pulse; one of a number of invented words
canaries:	wine from the Canary Islands
When Arthur . . . King:	first lines of a popular song
jordan:	chamber pot
calm:	qualm
sect:	here, sex
rascal:	a young deer
Your . . . ouches:	probably from a ballad; an ouch is a brooch or a scab
to serve . . . chambers:	military phrases with secondary sexual meanings
as rheumatic as two dry toasts:	the temperament was thought to be the result of the balance in each person of the four 'humours'. The Hostess means to refer to 'choleric' (the other three are sanguine, melancholic and phlegmatic), which is hot and dry, like toast
confirmities:	infirmities
merchant . . . stuff:	boat full of wine
Ancient:	ensign, standard-bearer
swaggering:	blustering
cheater:	cardsharper's decoy (not frightening)
Barbary hen:	guinea fowl (also a prostitute)
Pistol:	the word has a sexual innuendo, leading to a series of obscene puns
bung:	something that fills a hole; a pick-pocket
cuttle:	knife used for cutting purses
basket-hilt:	an old-fashioned sword
points:	laces (here meaning those used for tying on armour, implying that Pistol boasts of more than he can perform)
murder your ruff:	destroy your collar
stewed . . . cakes:	scraps of brothel-fare and pastry-cooks' throwouts, implying that Pistol lives off immoral earnings
occupy:	this word had acquired the sense of 'fornicate'

Pluto's ... lake: in classical mythology Pluto was the god of hell; 'lake' refers to the Stygian lake, one of the rivers of hell, the Styx

Erebus: the son of Chaos and Night in classical mythology

faitours: impostors

Hiren: (*i*) iron, or sword (*ii*) Irene, a character from a play. Pistol's diction is filled with scraps from old-style declamatory drama

Peesel: this is how Pistol's name was pronounced; it has an obscene meaning

aggravate: she means 'moderate'

jades: old horses (this line is from a play by Christopher Marlowe, a contemporary playwright)

Cerberus: in classical mythology a three-headed dog which guarded the gates of hell

Calipolis: a character from a play by George Peele, another contemporary playwright; the line is a paraphrase of one from a Peele play

Si ... contento: he means 'If fortune torments me, hope contents me' but the language is of Pistol's own invention; it resembles Italian

neaf: (*dialect*) hand

Galloway nags: (*i*) lively horses from south-west Scotland (*ii*) prostitutes

shove-groat shilling: meaning Pistol should be pushed out like a coin used in a game in which shillings were pushed up a wooden board

Shall ... imbrue: 'Shall we let blood' ('we' is the plural form used by kings)

Sisters Three: in classical mythology the three Fates: Clotho, Lachesis and Atropos

Hector ... Agamemnon ... Worthies: famous heroes

canvass: catch in a net (a term from hawking)

like a church: perhaps meaning Falstaff is immobile

Bartholomew: referring to a famous fair held on St Bartholomew's day, 24 August

foining: sword-thrusting (sexual innuendo)

pantler ... chipped bread: a pantryworker cutting the crusts off loaves

Tewksbury: Tewkesbury, a town in south-west England famed for its mustard

conger and fennel: an eel flavoured with a herb sauce

gambol: playful: all the pastimes mentioned are trivial

poll: hair

Saturn and Venus: planets representing old age and love

trigon, his man:	refers to the fiery-faced Bardolph, 'trigon' meaning the three fiery signs of the Zodiac, Aries, Leo and Sagittarius
candle-mine:	Falstaff is so gross that candles could be carved out of him
Gad's Hill:	a reference to a robbery committed by Falstaff (see *1 Henry IV*, II.2, II.4)
Lent:	a period of fasting when it was forbidden to eat meat
south ... vapor:	a wind bringing black clouds
peascod time:	early summer
blubbered:	her face stained with tears

Act III Scene 1

The king, making his first appearance, reveals in a long soliloquy that his crown has brought him worry, not contentment. He is unable to sleep and suffers feelings of guilt about his unlawful seizure of the crown from Richard II, who had rightly prophesied Henry's troubled reign. The king is reassured by Warwick, who also brings news that Owen Glendower, one of his foremost enemies, has died.

NOTES AND GLOSSARY:

cribs:	hovels
pallets:	beds (of poor quality)
hurly:	uproar
Gave him defiance ... into corruption:	these events are treated in Shakespeare's *Richard II*. The king here recalls, almost word for word, lines from that play, V.1.55–68
Figuring ... deceased:	reproducing the form of what has already passed
Glendower:	he is a rebel leader in *1 Henry IV*
unseasoned:	unusually late

Act III Scene 2

Two justices, Shallow and Silence, discuss country matters and reminisce. Shallow remembers his 'mad days' as a student with Falstaff, who then arrives, as expected, to recruit soldiers for the king's army. Falstaff is shown a number of potential recruits, but he bases his selection on whether or not each man can pay him a bribe. The nostalgic Shallow recalls old times with Falstaff, who, when alone, reveals that Shallow's youth was not the least adventurous.

NOTES AND GLOSSARY:

| **rood:** | cross |

black woosel:	blackbird (dark hair was considered a blemish at this time)
Inns o' Court:	where students studied law
Clement's Inn:	less select than the Inns of Court, but also teaching law
Cotsole:	the Cotswolds, a hilly region in the west of England
bona robas:	prostitutes
How:	how much for
John o' Gaunt:	Henry IV's father
clapped i' th' clout:	hit the target
twelve score:	two hundred and forty yards
forehand . . . half:	an almost impossible distance (280–290 yards) shooting straight at the target
Thereafter as they be:	according to their condition
esquire:	gentleman, ranked beneath a knight
tall:	brave
accommodated:	provided (it must have been a fashionable word at this time)
Prick him:	tick his name off the list
pricked:	(*i*) picked on (*ii*) soured or mouldy; there is also sexual innuendo
shadows . . . muster-book:	fictitious names in the register (whose salary Falstaff would draw)
thousands:	referring to lice
ringing in:	ringing the church bells
Windmill . . . fields:	a place in an area of London noted for its brothels
Hem, boys!:	a drinking cry
Corporate:	he means 'corporal'
four Harry . . . crowns:	a country way of counting out one pound (half Mouldy's offer)
thews:	muscles
motion . . . hammer:	very rapidly
gibbets . . . bucket:	probably the idea is 'swifter than the man hoisting the brewer's yoke on to his shoulders'
half-faced:	thin-faced
caliver:	a light firearm
traverse:	either 'walk across' or 'present arms'
chopped . . . shot:	dried up marksman
tester:	coin worth sixpence
Mile-end Green:	a drill-ground in London for citizens receiving military training
Arthur's show:	an annual archery show in which contestants took the names of Knights of the Round Table; Sir Dagonet was Arthur's fool

quiver:	nimble
fetch off:	trick
Turnbull Street:	a brothel area in London
the Turk's tribute:	the Sultan of Turkey exacted his tribute harshly
genius:	spirit
overscutched:	over-beaten
housewives:	pronounced 'hussies' (meaning whores)
his ... goodnights:	songs of his own invention
Vice's dagger:	thin wooden dagger carried by Vice, a figure in old morality plays
treble hautboy:	a small musical instrument
philosopher's two stones:	twice as lucrative as this stone, believed to have the power to change base metal to gold

Act IV Scene 1

The rebel leaders, now at the head of their army, hear of the Earl of Northumberland's desertion of their cause as the arrival of the king's forces is reported. The Earl of Westmorland enters and asks the rebels to state their grievances, which they do, claiming that war was their only option having been denied redress at court. Their demands are conveyed to Prince John who arrives with a promise that these demands would be met. However, as soon as the rebels have disbanded their army, Prince John arrests them on grounds of treason.

NOTES AND GLOSSARY:

hold ... quality:	accord with his rank
countenanced:	approved
good letters:	scholarship
figure:	symbolise
point of war:	bugle-call in the battle-field
we are ... for it:	the Archbishop uses this metaphor of bodily disorder to describe disorder in the State
articles:	formal listing
grate on:	harass
brother general:	addressing Westmorland as a fellow commander. Some editors place a comma after 'brother', which implies a reference to his actual brother, executed by Henry IV
unequal:	not impartial
signories:	estates (as reported in *Richard II*, IV.1.87–9)
armèd ... beavers:	lances at the ready, visors (of their helmets) down
warder:	mace (this act stopped the combat between Mowbray and Bolingbroke; see *Richard II*, I.3.118)

Hereford:	another name for the future Henry IV
Coventry:	the scene of the combat
policy:	statecraft of an unscrupulous kind
ken:	look
banks:	as of a river

were our royal faiths martyrs in love: if our love were so great that we would die for him

We shall ... partition: meaning that the wind that will blow on former rebels will be so harsh that good deeds will be dismissed with bad

weary ... grievances: tired of faulting such trivial misdemeanours

tables: notebook

Act IV Scene 2

This scene division is not in the Folio edition and is unnecessary – see summary for previous scene.

NOTES AND GLOSSARY:

iron:	(*i*) armoured (*ii*) merciless
opener and intelligencer:	interpreter and informant
dull workings:	limited perception
up-swarmed them:	made them swarm up
in common sense:	as all can see
parcels:	small details
Hydra:	a monster in classical mythology with many heads, killed by Hercules
against:	in expectation of
trains:	soldiers
capital:	punishable by death

Act IV Scene 3

Sir John Colevile, one of the scattered rebel army, yields to Falstaff, about which the fat knight is able to boast when John of Lancaster accuses him of dereliction of duty. Colevile is sent to execution and Prince John hastens to London where the king is reported to be sick. Falstaff, left alone, scornfully condemns the 'sober-blooded' prince, whom he contrasts with his 'hot and valiant' Prince Hal.

NOTES AND GLOSSARY:

condition:	rank
drops:	teardrops

my womb undoes me: the size of Falstaff's stomach makes his identity undeniable

foundered ... posts: lamed over 180 horses

fellow ... overcame: refers to the Roman Emperor Julius Caesar and the words he spoke on the defeat of King Pharnaces of Pontus

particular ballad else: a ballad about my feats otherwise (to be sold in the streets)

gilt ... me: counterfeits compared to me

cinders of the element: stars in heaven

come ... proof: stand much testing

green-sickness: anaemia, common in young girls

get: beget

inflammation: passions inflamed by alcohol

sherris-sack: white wine

cruddy: curd-like, thick

forgetive: inventing, creating

vital ... spirits: it was believed that three kinds of spirits (animal, natural and vital), carried in the blood, determined the nature of a man's body and mind

tempering: here, the act of rubbing wax between the fingers to soften it to take the impression of a seal

---

Act IV Scene 4

Awaiting news from the war, the ailing king promises to lead a crusade to the Holy Land. He is anxious about his heir, Prince Hal, who seems unfit for kingship. Despite the arrival of news of victories against his enemies his spirits are not raised and he has to be carried to his bed.

NOTES AND GLOSSARY:

invested: given authority

level: according

humorous: capricious

flaws congealed: snowstorms turned to ice

confound: destroy

working: exertion

suggestion: instigation (to evil)

aconitum: aconite or wolfsbane, a potent poison

fattest: richest

look beyond him: exaggerate his faults

mete: appraise

'Tis ... carrion: he will hardly forgo his pleasures, however corrupt

haunch: latter end

shrieve: sheriff

wrought the mure: made the wall

fear me: make me afraid

unfathered:	meaning unnaturally conceived
loathly:	of monstrous shape
flowed:	flooded. (Disturbances in nature were commonly believed to portend trouble in the State, such as the death of a king)

Act IV Scene 5

Prince Hal arrives at court and, thinking his father already dead, takes the crown from his bedside and departs. On awakening, the king accuses Hal of wishing him dead and prophesies a disorderly rule when he becomes king. The prince denies the charge and promises a 'noble change' from his former idleness. Reassured, the king gives him final advice on how best to rule, before being carried off to die.

NOTES AND GLOSSARY:

changes:	changes colour
ports:	gates (meaning eyes)
biggen:	nightcap
with safety:	while it protects
gates of breath:	lips
rigol:	circle
part:	act
bitter ... father:	the dying father gains only bitterness from his efforts for his son
sealed up:	confirmed
daggers:	in Shakespeare's source for this scene Prince Hal carries a dagger in his hand
form:	ceremony, law and order
dear:	dire, heart-felt
medicine potable:	'aurum potabile', a medicinal liquid containing gold
met:	implying that he did not seek the crown from Richard II
soil:	unsavoury aspects
argument:	plot of a play
successively:	by legitimate succession
griefs ... green:	grievances ... fresh
look/Too near unto:	examine too closely (and consider usurping)

Act V Scene 1

Justice Shallow, believing 'a friend i' th' court' is a great asset, gives Falstaff his best hospitality, but Falstaff mocks the rustic simplicity of

the household and looks forward to relating tales of Shallow's folly to
Prince Hal.

NOTES AND GLOSSARY:

By ... pie: a mild oath
precepts ... headland: orders ... unploughed strip between two
ploughed fields (Davy's duties are divided between
house and farm, and, we see later, legal business
also)
note: bill
cast: checked
kickshaws: fancy extras (French, *quelques choses*)
backbite ... backbitten: slander ... bitten by lice
countenance: favour
semblable coherence: close correspondence
curry: curry favour with
four terms ... two actions: Falstaff sees fashions changing six times a
year (the length of four law terms or two lawsuits)
intervallums: intervals
like ... up: creased like a wet cloth put away wrinkled

Act V Scene 2

After the king's death the nobles and court officers are fearful of changes
under the new king, especially the Lord Chief Justice who had been a
severe critic of Prince Hal. Henry V's magnanimity, however, dispels
these fears. He reinstates the Lord Chief Justice and directs him to be 'as
a father to my youth'.

NOTES AND GLOSSARY:

heavy issue: grieving sons
he: whoever is
strike ... sort: give way to base people
our argument: the subject of our speech
Amurath: a Turkish Sultan who had his brothers murdered
when he succeeded his father, Selim II, in 1574
Rate: berate, scold
easy: insignificant. (In this well known legend, the Lord
Chief Justice sent Hal to prison for striking him; see
I.2.53–4 and 195–7)
Lethe: a river in Hades (the Greek underworld) which
caused forgetfulness if drunk from
use the person of: represent
workings ... body: activities carried out as by your representative
propose: imagine

wild into his grave: my wildness is buried with him
affections: appetites
accite: summon
state: high-ranking subjects
consigning to: endorsing

Act V Scene 3

After the meal, planned in Act V Scene 1, Shallow and Silence, now somewhat drunk, entertain Falstaff until Pistol arrives with news of Prince Hal's succession. Falstaff, anticipating great favour from the new king, rushes to London proclaiming 'blessed are they that have been my friends, and woe to my Lord Chief Justice'.

NOTES AND GLOSSARY:

pippin: type of apple
graffing: grafting
caraways: caraway seeds or cakes containing them
husband: steward
quoth 'a: said he
Proface! a formula before a meal meaning 'may it do you good' (French, *bon prou vous fasse*)
want: lack
Shrovetide: period of feasting just before Lent
twice and once: a formula suggesting frequency
leather-coats: russet apples (having rough skins)
leman: lover
a mile to th' bottom: Silence claims he could drain his 'cup' in one swallow even if it were a mile deep
cabileros: fine fellows
pottle-pot: a two-quart tankard
A ... out: he won't drop out
done me right: meaning 'matched me drink for drink'
Do ... Samingo: lines from a drinking song. Drinking a deep draught while kneeling entitled one to be called 'knight'
but goodman Puff: except for yeoman Puff (who was presumably even fatter than Falstaff)
A foutre for: a crude expression of contempt
Africa: associated with gold
O base ... thereof: here Falstaff imitates Pistol's manner to try to communicate. Cophetua is the name of an African king in a well-known ballad
Robin ... John: a scrap from a ballad, referring to three famous outlaws

Helicons:	Pistol claims to be inspired by the Muses, in contrast to Silence whom he calls a 'dunghill cur' for competing with him in verse
baffled:	prevented, confounded
Besonian:	ignoramus (from the Spanish *bisoño*, raw recruit)
do this:	make an insulting gesture, called a 'fig', by placing the thumb between the index and third fingers
Let . . . lungs:	a reference from classical mythology either to Tityrus (whose liver was eaten by vultures) or to Prometheus (who received the same treatment from an eagle)
Where . . . led:	a line from a poem, now lost

Act V Scene 4

Mistress Quickly and Doll Tearsheet, suspected of involvement in a tavern-killing, are arrested and dragged off to court.

NOTES AND GLOSSARY:

whipping-cheer:	plenty of whipping (the usual punishment for prostitution)
about:	(*i*) because of (*ii*) in the company of
Nut-hook:	a hooked stick, applied to the beadle because he catches hold of objects
tripe-visaged:	a face like a tripe (pock-marked)
the child I go with:	a lie to escape chastisement, but the beadle implies that the 'child' is no more than a cushion stuffed up her skirt (see lines 14–15)
thin man in a censer:	a flat, decorative figure on a perfuming-pan, who obviously looks very thin
swinged:	beaten
bluebottle:	the beadles wore blue uniforms
forswear half-kirtles:	give up wearing skirts
knight-errant:	meaning 'night-errant' (one who sins at night)
right . . . might:	a typical reversal of intended meaning
atomy:	she means 'anatomy' (skeleton)

Act V Scene 5

Falstaff and his associates line the route of Henry V's coronation procession. Confident of the king's favour he promises to secure Doll's release, but when he presents himself to the king he is rejected. Falstaff's reassurance to Shallow (to whom he owes money) that he will be called for in private seems ill-founded when the Lord Chief Justice sends him to prison.

NOTES AND GLOSSARY:

rushes:	strewn on the ground (as a mark of deference)
leer:	glance slyly (indecorous, as he should bow his head)
shift me:	change of clothes
semper ... *est*:	the two Latin mottoes mean 'always the same' and 'without this, nothing'
all in every part:	of unclear meaning, this resembles an English motto, "'Tis all in all and all in every part', expressing absolute perfection
liver:	supposedly the seat of the passions
Helen:	an absurd comparison with the legendary Helen of Troy, famed for her beauty
mechanical:	working-class
Alecto:	one of the Furies in Greek mythology, who had snakes twined in their hair and were agents of revenge
imp:	obsolete word for a descendant of a noble line
riots:	riotous behaviour (a word used throughout Shakespeare's histories to denote irresponsible behaviour)
colour:	(*i*) appearance (*ii*) noose (Shallow infers that Falstaff will be hanged rather than favoured)
Si ... *contenta*:	see note to II.4.176
ere ... **France:**	relating back to the king's advice to Hal (see IV.5.213–14)
civil swords:	ones used in the recent civil war

Epilogue

Written in three sections, the first two repeating the conventional appeal for applause, the third, possibly added at a later date, containing the promise of a sequel 'with Sir John in it' (although Falstaff does not appear in Shakespeare's sequel, *Henry V*).

NOTES AND GLOSSARY:

doubt:	fear
venture ... break:	business venture ... go bankrupt
Bate me some:	forgive part of my debt
Katherine:	whom Henry marries in *Henry V*
Oldcastle:	the original name for Falstaff, altered by Shakespeare probably because descendants of the historical Oldcastle complained

Part 3

Commentary

Date and sources

The original name for Falstaff was Oldcastle, but early in 1597 descendants of the original Oldcastle complained about Shakespeare's use of their name. As traces of the name Oldcastle still remain in *Henry IV Part 2*, either all or part of it was written at some time between the early performances of *Henry IV Part 1* in 1596 and the protest. It is most likely that Part 2 was written immediately after Part 1, and that the two plays were performed on successive occasions. However, we only know for certain that it was completed before the next play in the sequence, *Henry V*, was begun early in 1599.

The two interweaving elements of *2 Henry IV*, which can be conveniently labelled comical and historical, have as their main sources two separate works. The comic scenes draw on an anonymous play called *The Famous Victories of Henry the Fifth*, not published until 1598 but performed over ten years previously in a fuller state than survives into print. The historical scenes are mainly based on Ralph Holinshed's *Chronicle of England* (1587 edition), which has a chapter on Henry IV entitled 'King Henry's Unquiet Reign'. Knowledge of Shakespeare's sources is very useful, for by observing what he selects or omits, what he accepts or alters, we can observe his interpretation of a particular character or historical event. For example, he chooses to leave out those details from *The Famous Victories* which present Prince Henry as a law-breaker, ambitious for his father's crown, and emphasises his submission to the law. Instead of the prince entering the king's sick-chamber with a dagger in his hand, Shakespeare changes his source and merely has the king suspect, 'Thou hidest a thousand daggers in thy thoughts' (IV.5.107).

Shakespeare also departs from Holinshed in the way he presents, for example, the characters of Prince John and the Earl of Northumberland. In Holinshed Northumberland is not a coward, and Prince John does not cheat the rebels. Shakespeare made these changes, which tend to portray both the rebels and the royal family in a worse light, presumably altering history to gain dramatic effects and to reinforce his interpretation of it. Thus he reduces the five year gap between the battle of Shrewsbury and the defeat of Scrope's rebellion to a few weeks, and almost removes the eight year gap between the king's victory over the rebels and his death, by which means Henry's reign does indeed appear 'uneasy'.

The relationship between the two parts of *Henry IV*

Before discussing the nature of Part 2 of *Henry IV* the student needs to think of its relationship to its predecessor Part 1. Some critics think that Part 1 and Part 2 make one single play, and are 'two only because they are too long to be one', as Dr Johnson wrote. If this is true, you need to read Part 1, just as you would need to read the first two and a half acts of a five act play. The main argument in favour of this theory is that the climax of Part 2, the resolution of the relations between Prince Henry (Hal), Falstaff and the king, is also the natural climax of Part 1. 'Banish plump Jack and banish all the world' (II.4.473–4), Falstaff's words in Part 1, have their natural counterpart in Hal's words of banishment in Part 2: 'I know thee not old man' (V.5.50). The main argument against is that each part does work on the stage as a separate play, which suggests that they are coherent unities.

The two parts have very different natures. Part 1 is more light-hearted; the characters are livelier and more attractive, and Falstaff, in particular, provides a holiday spirit which counteracts the uneasiness about Henry's troubled reign. Besides being a more sombre and disturbing play, Part 2 seems designed to repeat in a contrasting way rather than simply continue the action of Part 1, as would be expected of a sequel. In both parts Shakespeare bases the historical part of the action on a rebellion, but the leaders of both rebel and royal forces in Part 1 are much more heroic, individualised and colourful (Hal's victory over Hotspur in Part 1 contrasts sharply with Prince John's trickery in Part 2). In both parts the other main element in the plot is the development of Hal. In Part 1 he emerges from a damaged reputation, caused by associating with Falstaff, as the hero of the battle of Shrewsbury. In Part 2 this reformation is deliberately unstressed so that Shakespeare can repeat the situation of Hal having to choose between alternative ways (represented in Part 1 by the courageous Hotspur and Falstaff, in Part 2 by Falstaff and the Lord Chief Justice). In Part 2, however, Hal hardly seems tempted by Falstaff's licentious way of living, which he enters into the spirit of in Part 1. Shakespeare also goes to a lot of trouble in Part 2 to remind us of the content of Part 1 (and of the first play in the sequence, *Richard II*) which would be superfluous in a single ten act play. It may be that Shakespeare only decided to write Part 2 after the success of Part 1 on the stage, but it is at least as likely that he envisaged a sequel when he began Part 1. The safest attitude for a student to take to this problem is to approach Part 2 as a separate play, which, because of the nature of history or Shakespeare's conception of history, grows out of events recorded in Part 1.

The nature of the play

2 Henry IV is not a straightforward play. Some critics have linked it to a group known as Shakespeare's 'problem plays'. These plays are characterised by their presentation of characters and moral issues in a way that leaves the audience uneasy and unsure how to respond. We find it difficult to know how to respond to much of *2 Henry IV*, whether we should be critical of or sympathetic towards characters and actions. This is particularly true of the two moral crises of the play, the tricking of the rebels by Prince John and the rejection of Falstaff by Prince Henry, both of which have been argued about by critics for centuries. We may be able to see the political necessity of such acts, but, neverthless, feel that Prince John's action is dishonourable and his brother's heartless. We find it hard to sympathise fully with any of the characters or to take sides in the civil conflict. The king, it could be argued, was himself a rebel against *his* king, Richard II, and therefore no better than the Archbishop of York and the other rebel leaders. But the rebels seem to have no clear cause to fight for other than their own personal advantage and hence lose our sympathy also. Falstaff's desire to use the influence he thinks he has over Prince Henry for his own benefit, and Prince Henry's casting aside an old comrade whom he had used for his pleasure, are typical of the unpleasant personal relations in this play. It is a play without love, in which friends use or betray each other. In this moral anarchy God's influence is nowhere apparent. Statesmen are guided by political necessity:

> Are these things then necessities?
> Then let us meet them like necessities.

> (III.1.88–9)

These words of Henry IV are paralleled by Falstaff's code of conduct:

> A good wit will make use of anything; I will turn diseases to commodity.

> (I.2.249–51)

It is not surprising in such a world that Prince Henry should be reluctant to express a loving care for his sick father because he would immediately be suspected of hypocrisy (II.2.44–53). The impression we receive from this play is of disease and disorder. Moreover, the wide scope of the play makes it appear that the whole of society, from top to bottom, is suffering from this disease and disorder. We move from court to tavern, from country house to battlefield, between scenes of everyday life and scenes of lofty State affairs, and wherever we are taken the dominant mood is in some way unpleasant. This scope is in time as well as place. We are continually reminded of events in the past and we are also projected into the future, and neither memories nor prophecies are free from a sense of disorder in the State (see, for example, King Henry's speech, IV.5.178-9). The apparently universal nature of the problems facing the king helps to explain why he is so sick at heart, and why the emergence of his son as a good ruler is so vital for the country.

The structure of the play

2 Henry IV has two main actions. One concerns the fortunes of Falstaff and the other concerns the conflict between the government and the rebellion led by the Archbishop of York. Besides these two actions Shakespeare also makes use of the structural pattern of the medieval morality plays (discussed on page 15) by placing Prince Henry between Falstaff and the Lord Chief Justice as alternatives for him to choose between. Despite these three structural elements in the play, however, there is little development of the plot, little suspense in the narrative. As the audience can see Prince Henry turning against Falstaff, we can guess that his fortunes will decline from the beginning of the play. We can also foresee that the rebellion will fail, both because the rebel leaders are so vague and confused and because Northumberland, their strongest ally, decides to withdraw his support in Act II Scene 3. The morality pattern similarly lacks development as Prince Henry seems to have made his choice (in favour of law and order and against Falstaff) by the start of the play, and, in contrast with the medieval morality plays, he rarely meets with the two figures contending for his soul. For these reasons the climaxes of *2 Henry IV* are reduced in impact as the surprise value is lessened: the rebellion fizzles out as does the life of the old king. The rejection of Falstaff has been long prepared for and it shocks us only because of the harsh and public nature of the new king's words.

Shakespeare's greatest structural achievement in the play is his interweaving of the comical and historical material. His simple structural device is to alternate between these two worlds, one following after the other in a sequence which is unbroken until Act V Scene 4. On the surface there is a clear separation, even an opposition, between the two worlds: court against tavern, authority against licence, seriousness against levity, verse against prose. However, there is a continuity of imagery and themes which draws the two worlds together. Both are aspects of the troubled nature of Henry's reign; both reflect disorder and disease; both come under the arms of the law (the rebels executed and Falstaff imprisoned) and both show a lack of moral principles (for example, Prince John cheats the rebels and Falstaff cheats Mistress Quickly).

The effect of this inter-relationship of such wide-ranging material is to give the impression that the entire country is suffering from the same problems, or that whatever a man's station in life might be, he will be affected by disorder in the State. The material which Shakespeare presents in the historical scenes is contrasted, paralleled or inverted in the comic scenes that come before or after. For example, a limping, aged and ranting Earl of Northumberland occupies the centre of the stage in Act I Scene 1 and is replaced in the next scene by a limping, aged and ranting comic counterpart in the figure of Falstaff. In these and other contrasting scenes Shakespeare invites us to judge each scene by values established in the contrasting scene. In this way Northumberland's excessive passion appears more ridiculous and Falstaff's self-indulgent complaints appear more trivial and irresponsible.

Age and disease: Imagery in the play

A close reading of *2 Henry IV* will reveal that certain images keep reappearing regardless of change of scene, and these key images reveal the major concerns of the dramatist and make a very significant contribution to the overall impression that the play makes. The dominant images in *2 Henry IV* are those concerned with age and disease, which are a vehicle for the moral and physical decay which characterises this play. The age and sickness of the characters reflect disharmony in the State, just as, the Elizabethans believed, disorder in the State disturbs other elements in the universe. Thus the king's fatal sickness disrupts nature's harmony:

> The people fear me, for they do observe
> Unfathered heirs and loathly births of nature.
> The seasons change their manners, as the year
> Had found some months asleep and leaped them over.
>
> (IV.4.121–4)

The body, the State and the universe only moved in harmony when man remained obedient to God's Law. The emphasis on age and disease in *2 Henry IV* is a sign that this law has been broken. The king, the arch-rebel Northumberland and the comic knight Falstaff are physically decaying, but this is only an outward sign of moral ills. There are also old and decaying men such as Justice Shallow, who have left the best of their lives behind them and live mainly in the past. Prince Henry is the only major character in the play (except for the symbol of Law, the Lord

Chief Justice) who has any future to look forward to, in a country which has rid itself of the diseased and aged generation which was implicated with the deposition and murder of King Richard II. The disease seems to stem from Richard's death, as the Archbishop says:

> we are all diseased,
> And with our surfeiting and wanton hours
> Have brought ourselves into a burning fever,
> And we must bleed for it; of which disease
> Our late King Richard being infected died.

(IV.1.54–8)

King Henry also thinks of England as a diseased country:

> Then you perceive the body of our kingdom
> How foul it is, what rank diseases grow,
> And with what danger, near the heart of it.

(III.1.38–40)

and he relates this disease back to Richard's deposition (see III.1.72–3). He also sees Prince Henry as part of his sickness: 'This part of his conjoins with my disease' (IV.5.65).

This metaphorical disease is also visible on the stage. Northumberland appears leaning on a crutch and with his head bandaged. Falstaff suffers from gout and limps. Judging from the Lord Chief Justice's catalogue of his ailments he must appear physically grotesque:

> Have you not a moist eye, a dry hand, a yellow cheek, a white beard, a decreasing leg, an increasing belly? Is not your voice broken, your wind short, your chin double, your wit single, and every part about you blasted with antiquity?

(I.2.182–6)

The king is also visibly ill and actually appears on the stage on a sick-bed. In contrast Prince Henry is youthful and healthy, and it is significant that his rejection of Falstaff is made in terms of the latter's age and infirmity (see V.5.50–7).

In the comic and low-life scenes age and disease are associated with lechery, which draws together the moral and physical disorder of Falstaff's world. There is something disgusting and unnatural about the combination of lust, old age and infection that we find in the tavern scenes. The relationship between sex and disorder is particularly apparent in the language of Pistol, which is both violent and full of sexual innuendo. The relationship between sex and disease is embodied in Doll Tearsheet. She is 'sick of a calm' (II.4.36) on her first entrance and is a carrier of disease, as Falstaff says: 'you help to make the diseases, Doll. We catch of you, Doll, we catch of you' (II.4.44–6). In the person of Justice Shallow lust is combined with impotence, and the old man has to invent sexual encounters which never took place. Just as for Falstaff, death waits around the corner for Shallow, but he refuses to accept the part of an old man.

Law and order and individual freedom

In our age political and social debate has centred on the conflict between State influence (the forces of law and order) and the freedom of the individual. This conflict is also at the heart of *2 Henry IV*. Law, in the person of the Lord Chief Justice, is opposed by lawlessness, in the person of Falstaff. Falstaff considers himself above the law. 'You speak as having power to do wrong' (II.1.128-9), the Lord Chief Justice says to him, and towards the end of the play he boasts that 'The laws of England are at my commandment' (V.3.134-5).

We are told that Falstaff has committed a robbery at a place called Gad's Hill (I.2.151) and we see him illegally misusing his powers as a recruiting officer for the king. He is arrested in Act II and again in Act V, and his two female friends are also arrested (V.4). These facts put together with his repeated arguments with the Lord Chief Justice place Falstaff as the play's major opponent to law and order. Rebellion is also linked with lawlessness from the start of the play:

> The times are wild; contention, like a horse
> Full of high feeding, madly hath broke loose
> And bears down all before him.

> (I.1.9-11)

Northumberland's words here and his passionate outburst, 'Let heaven kiss earth! . . . Let order die' (I.1.153-4), present rebellion as upsetting the laws of Nature, whereas Falstaff rejects man-made laws. The Archbishop of York himself admits to the unnaturalness of rebellion:

> The time misordered doth, in common sense,
> Crowd us and crush us to this monstrous form
> To hold our safety up.

> (IV.2.33-5)

He claims, however, that the disorder stems from the king, who admits privately to his son and heir that the troubles of his reign relate back to his crime of usurpation:

> God knows, my son,
> By what by-paths and indirect crooked ways
> I met this crown, and I myself know well
> How troublesome it sat upon my head.

> (IV.5.183-6)

Prince Henry's irresponsible or individualistic behaviour also threatens to upset law and order in the country. Henry IV prophesies the end of law after his son's succession:

> Pluck down my officers, break my decrees . . . .
> Have you a ruffian that will swear, drink, dance,
> Revel the night, rob, murder, and commit
> The oldest sins the newest kinds of ways?
> Be happy, he will trouble you no more.

(IV.5.118–28)

Prince Henry's bad rule is here seen specifically as overthrowing the law and it is significant that his reformation is demonstrated by taking the Lord Chief Justice as his new 'father' (V.2.118) and by summoning Parliament, which is the law-making body in the kingdom.

Henry V in this way submits his individual will to the control of public authority (see V.2.120–1), and he must inevitably reject the play's symbol of uncontrolled individualism, Falstaff. Prince Henry's individualism is much more apparent in *1 Henry IV*, but traces of it can be found in *2 Henry IV*, as, for example, when he and Poins dress up as tavern waiters in order to spy on Falstaff (II.4). The main reason why we feel regret at Falstaff's banishment is that individualism is not only associated with lawlessness, which a country's leader must reject, but it is also linked to a zest for life, which those at court, particularly Prince John but Prince Henry also, seem to have lost. Prince Henry's first words in the play are, 'Before God, I am exceeding weary' (II.2.1), which is similar in mood to King Henry's world-weary speech, the last two lines of which are:

> Then happy low, lie down!
> Uneasy lies the head that wears a crown.

(III.1.30–1)

In contrast with this, Falstaff, despite his age, is full of vitality and lives life to the full:

> I am only old in judgement and understanding; and he that will caper with me for a thousand marks, let him lend me the money, and have at him!

(I.2.192–5)

He gravitates to Prince Henry because he recognises a similar spirit in him (see V.1.71–3 and contrast IV.3.87–8) but fails to realise that the prince had stifled his individualism to prepare himself for the duties of kingship.

Falstaff and his rejection

Sir John Falstaff has always been considered the most memorable character in *2 Henry IV*, but there has been wide disagreement about him. Those who see him as representing 'Humanity' condemn his rejection by Henry V; those for whom he represents 'Vice' or 'Disorder' applaud the rejection. Those who admire Falstaff will dislike Prince Henry: those who admire Prince Henry will dislike Falstaff. Falstaff appeals to the holiday spirit in us, while Prince Henry's accession, which brings the holiday to an end, appeals to that part of us which wants firm authority to keep our reckless holiday spirit in control. Our mixed feelings about Falstaff are also the result of his role in the play. He dominates the low-life scenes as a fat, clown-like figure, but he is also a knight and a captain in the king's army, so he has a place in the higher ranks of society. He exists to be laughed at, but at the same time we have to take him seriously as a threat to the welfare of the country. He spans both of the actions in the play, the comical and the historical. He figures in Lord Bardolph's report of the battle of Shrewsbury (I.1.19–20); he appears at Gaultree Forest after the rebellion has collapsed and he is also at the centre of the rejection in which the two actions are brought together.

In order to prepare us for the rejection Shakespeare seems to have decided to make Falstaff less attractive than he is in Part 1 of *Henry IV*. In Part 1 he is a harmless and witty rogue, but in Part 2 his wit is less impressive and he is no longer harmless. He has become more pompous, self-satisfied and obsessed with his rank and reputation. This vain arrogance is apparently the result of a widespread belief that he was a hero at the battle of Shrewsbury. Even the Lord Chief Justice has accepted this false report, saying to Falstaff:

> Your day's service at Shrewsbury hath a little gilded over your night's exploit on Gad's Hill.
>
> (I.2.150–1)

Falstaff's boast, 'I would to God my name were not so terrible to the enemy as it is' (I.2.219–20), would seem to be true, as Colevile, a famous rebel, surrenders to him with the words, 'I think you are Sir John Falstaff, and in that thought yield me' (IV.3.16–17).

Falstaff wins our affection in Part 1 because he is able to laugh at himself, but in Part 2 he takes himself seriously and we laugh at his folly rather than his wit. At times we do not laugh at all, as his behaviour is downright unpleasant. He regularly abuses friendship and hospitality, viewing personal relations only in terms of what he can extract from them. Thus Shallow is seen as a small fish and therefore fit prey for Falstaff, a big fish:

> If the young dace be a bait for the old pike, I see no reason in the law of
> nature but I may snap at him.
>
> (III.2.318–20)

Falstaff is not only less pleasant and less witty, he is also far more
disorderly and is in physical as well as moral decline. As the play
progresses his threat to the well-being of the country becomes more
apparent. An Elizabethan audience would have been shocked by a man
who announced himself as a destructive force, 'like a sow that hath
overwhelmed all her litter but one' (I.2.11–12), and then claimed that
'the laws of England are at my commandment' (V.3.134–5).

It is possible to see Falstaff as being in body and mind a monstrous
creation, but such a view omits one factor which makes other characters
in the play and members of the audience alike forgive his faults, and this
factor is Falstaff's charm. His speech has a persuasive power which
dazzles those who listen. Even Prince Henry is drawn, until he is made
king, by Falstaff's power to charm, and he goes to spy on him in disguise
at least partly because of the pleasure he takes in Falstaff's performance.
Poins realises the effect Falstaff's speech can have on the Prince:

> My lord, he will drive you out of your revenge and turn all to
> merriment, if you take not the heat.
>
> (II.4.293–4)

Similarly, Hostess Quickly's desire for revenge is removed by Falstaff
once he has her private attention (II.1.135–61), and he later charms
Justice Shallow into giving him a thousand pounds and Colevile into
giving up his person. Only Prince John, who is unnaturally cold, and the
Lord Chief Justice, who is less a person than a symbol of the law, do not
fall under Falstaff's spell. Throughout Parts 1 and 2 of *Henry IV* he is
able to talk his way out of awkward situations, but the greatest test of his
powers of survival comes in the rejection scene. Here, for the first time,
he is crushed on the stage; his charm deserts him; the spell is broken:
'being awaked I do despise my dream' (V.5.54), King Henry V says.
Audiences have always been sad to see this larger-than-life figure
reduced in this way. Falstaff is related to what was called the 'Lord of
Misrule', who was allowed special privileges on certain holidays when
the laws governing society were put aside. But the reign of the Lord of
Misrule ended with the holiday. His influence, like Falstaff's, could only
be temporary.

Prince Henry

Prince Henry makes only five brief appearances but, because *2 Henry IV*
centres on his choice between Falstaff and the Lord Chief Justice, he can
be considered to be the hero of the play. In his first appearance (II.2) we

see the conflict within him between the demands of his position as heir to the crown and his personal preference for low things like 'small beer', which are not fitting for a man of his 'high blood' (II.2.3). In the play it is Falstaff whom we associate with alcoholic drink. Moreover, the reason he gives for his admiration of Prince Henry is that the prince had developed a taste for 'sack', a type of wine which Falstaff sees as a true test of character. It would appear, then, that the two men share common tastes, but even at this early point in the play Prince Henry has decided to erase his reputation for loose living: 'Let the end try the man' (II.2.44), he says to his friend Poins.

We next see the prince in disguise spying on Falstaff. This is the only time we see them on stage together before the rejection scene. This tavern scene is partly intended to show us why the rejection has to take place, as Falstaff is presented at his most debauched level in the play; drunk, lecherous and squabbling in 'vile company' (II.2.46). Prince Henry's words at the end of the scene reveal both self-disgust and disgust with Falstaff's way of living:

> By heaven, Poins, I feel me much to blame,
> So idly to profane the precious time.

> (II.4.356–7)

The prince's revulsion has to make a lasting impression on the audience as he does not reappear for two acts, and when we next see him we know that he will never set foot in a tavern with Falstaff again. He has become a very serious young man, with his eyes fixed on the future government of his country. The king, like Falstaff, is ignorant of this reformation. He accuses his son of wishing him dead in order to begin a lawless reign. In his reply Prince Henry promises to 'show th' incredulous world: The noble change that I have purposèd!' (IV.5.154–5)

His first three appearances in the play, as we have seen, prepare the audience for a choice to be made between the duties of high office and the wild life of Prince Henry's past. His final two appearances confirm the choice which has been implied before. He shows his obedience to authority by taking the Lord Chief Justice 'as a father to my youth' (V.2.118), and speaking as King Henry V, promises that England will rank 'with the best-governed nation' (V.2.137). Falstaff is now doomed. His rejection in the final scene is the logical conclusion to the stages we have seen Prince Henry pass through during the play. Shakespeare's careful preparation should make Prince Henry's words to Falstaff appear less harsh and shocking to the audience. Much depends on how sympathetically or critically a director of the play decides to present Henry V at this point.

Shakespeare's sources and popular tradition accepted Henry V as the model of ideal kingship, who brought order and glory to England.

History showed that a strong and popular monarch was needed at a time of civil disorder and Prince Henry is presented in *2 Henry IV* as a cure for England's ills. What Shakespeare also wants us to be aware of, however, is the personal sacrifice that the role of kingship demands. Henry V has to close off part of himself in order to govern well. He must become cold and practical and be guided by law not personal preference. Many readers lose sympathy with Prince Henry as he becomes more like his brother John, whom 'a man cannot make . . . laugh' (IV.3.87–8), but as we see in Shakespeare's other history plays such as *Richard II*, there is grave danger to the State when a king allows sentiment to interfere in government.

King Henry IV

Henry IV is not the central character of the play which bears his name, which is unusual in Shakespeare. Nevertheless he is a strongly drawn character with a well defined personality and role in the play. One indication of the depth of the dramatist's interest in King Henry is the fact that he lets him speak alone on the stage. Soliloquies were used to great effect by Shakespeare to reveal the inner workings of a character's mind (notice the revelatory nature of Prince Henry's speech when he is alone except for his unconscious father (IV.5.22–48)). Henry IV's soliloquy is vital for an understanding of his character, as he is a shrewd politician who is only likely to reveal the truth in private. He reveals that his mind is so troubled that he cannot sleep, a conventional indication of feelings of guilt, and considers the lowest of his subjects to be better off than he. Here Shakespeare touches upon a theme which recurs throughout his history plays: the gap between the great office of kingship, symbolised by the crown, and the imperfect human being who bears this burden of absolute power:

> Then happy low, lie down!
> Uneasy lies the head that wears a crown.

(III.1.30–1)

Henry's troubled mind reflects his troubled kingdom, and the cause of both is the same: his seizure of the crown from the lawful king of England, Richard II. He feels guilty for this crime, and his reign has been undermined by its being founded on an illegitimate act. He admits this in private conversation with Prince Henry:

> God knows, my son,
> By what by-paths and indirect crooked ways
> I met this crown, and I myself know well
> How troublesome it sat upon my head.

(IV.5.183–6)

The disorder of his mind is paralleled by disorder in his body, both of which are worsened by the conduct of Prince Henry, which he sees as part of his punishment:

This part of his conjoins with my disease
And helps to end me.

(IV.5.65–6)

He is a man who cannot escape from his past, and thinking that the crown is about to be passed on to a lawless successor, sees even the future darkened by his crime against Richard II.

Henry IV is one of a number of characters who have become old and decayed since Part 1 of *Henry IV*, but his physical decline is not matched by a decline in political wisdom. He won the crown and he keeps it by being a skilled and ruthless statesman. He is an opportunist who acts according to what is necessary to maintain power, rather than according to what is morally right. He states his code of conduct in the lines:

Are these things then necessities?
Then let us meet them like necessities.

(III.1.88–9)

Even at the point of death his advice to Prince Henry directs him not towards virtue but towards political expediency, not the ideals of kingship but the harsh reality. The prince is told he must wage war, not for any cause, but to distract the masses (IV.5.212–15). It is typical of such a king that his seemingly religious desire to visit the Holy Land (IV.4.3–4) has, in fact, a political motivation (IV.5.209–12).

The other characters

Falstaff, Prince Henry and King Henry IV are the only characters who are developed in any detail, but there is a host of lively minor characters in this play. Many of these characters are given tag names which suggest physical or mental characteristics such as Pistol, Doll Tearsheet, Shallow, Shadow, Mouldy and Fang and Snare (the two officers who try to arrest Falstaff). These tag names are sometimes misleading, but they indicate that Shakespeare intended these to be flat characters, incapable of development and usually limited to a single distinctive characteristic. These comic characters make a lasting impression, which is not the case with the minor characters from the historical scenes, whether rebels or of the king's party. Only Prince John and the Lord Chief Justice warrant separate attention; the remaining characters will be considered in three groupings: the rebels, the Boar's Head characters and the Gloucestershire characters.

Prince John

Prince John is brought into prominence by his shocking and unscrupulous handling of the rebellion. His unheroic trickery makes a significant contrast with Part 1 of *Henry IV* in which the rebellion is put down by heroic acts of physical bravery. With Prince John the medieval age of heroic chivalry has passed and gone. His concern is with success, not with honour; with political expediency, not with moral principles. He only uses the name of God to cloak an act of cynical treachery:

> God, and not we, hath safely fought today.
>
> (IV.2.121)

So he speaks after breaking his oath to the rebels. His character is cold, efficient and calculating. Falstaff shrewdly says of him 'nor a man cannot make him laugh' (IV.3.87–8). His function in the play is to show with stark clarity the gap that exists at this time between politics and morality. This influences our opinion of the entire royal family including Prince Henry, whose policies he is linked with at the end of the play (V.5.100–12).

The Lord Chief Justice

The Lord Chief Justice does not develop as a character, nor has he a particularly distinctive personality. His significance lies in what he represents, which can be called either Law, Justice or Authority. As the main opponent to Falstaff in the play he has to be quick-witted, intelligent and authoritative, or else he would be overwhelmed in the wit combats which they have (I.2, II.1). In fact, Falstaff comes off worse when they meet and is made to appear foolish. The Lord Chief Justice's strength lies in his integrity, a quality that is made all the more striking in this play which is noticeably lacking in it. His integrity is such that he was prepared to risk his office and even his life by sending Prince Henry to prison for striking him (V.2.77–83). Shakespeare clearly intends his 'bold, just, and impartial spirit' (V.2.116) to shine like a beacon, exposing corruption and guiding the heir to the throne. His words are a combination of wisdom, honesty and force:

> Sweet Princes, what I did I did in honour,
> Led by th'impartial conduct of my soul.
> And never shall you see that I will beg
> A raggèd and forestalled remission.
>
> (V.2.35–8)

Here, with great dignity, he refuses to curry favour with the new king, but he is not a pompous speaker, and is able to tackle Falstaff in his own style of language (see II.1.107–15).

The rebels

The presentation of the Scrope rebellion in *2 Henry IV* bears a marked resemblance to a revolt by Catholics in northern England which took place in 1569, a fact which would have given it added relevance for an Elizabethan audience. Interest in the rebels themselves, however, must have been slight as they are an unimpressive and scarcely distinguished group of individuals. They are not sympathetically portrayed, having no apparent cause for revolt other than self-interest (see IV.1.53–87). They are political opportunists who are taking advantage of Henry IV's troubled reign to force him to adopt policies which would be more favourable to them. The archbishop speaks and acts like a politician, not a man of God. His discussions with the other rebels are not concerned with justification of rebellion but with their means and chances of success. Mowbray, Hastings and Lord Bardolph (not to be confused with red-nosed Bardolph, Falstaff's friend) are pale, insignificant characters. It seems fitting that their rebellion should collapse so feebly. All the rebel leaders are vague and uncertain. They use fine-sounding words and love to speechify but they seem more concerned with the manner than the content of what they say. We never *really* know why they are up in arms against their king. The folly of their rebellion is emphasised by Colevile's unnecessary submission to Falstaff. They each naively misjudge the nature of the men with whom they are dealing.

Closely identified with the rebels and yet not an active participant in the rebellion is the Earl of Northumberland. He is depicted as both reckless and cowardly. Like the other rebels he appears to have insufficient grounds for such a terrible act as rebellion. His motives are personal, based on a passion for revenge for the death of his son, the valiant Hotspur. Controlled by neither reason nor honour Northumberland forms with Falstaff the twin sources of disorder in the play. He longs for chaos:

Let heaven kiss earth! Now let not Nature's hand
Keep the wild flood confined! Let order die!   (I.1.153–4)

Like Henry IV, Northumberland is an old man who is inseparably bound to the past. Their shared guilt in Richard II's downfall influences the rest of their lives. They can only live out the prophecy which Richard made at his deposition:

'Northumberland, thou ladder by the which
My cousin Bolingbroke ascends my throne . . .
The time shall come' – thus did he follow it –
'The time will come that foul sin, gathering head,
Shall break into corruption'.   (*Richard II*, III.1.66–73)

Northumberland's cowardice in the play, in fleeing to Scotland to preserve his life, is not historically accurate. In Shakespeare's sources the archbishop moved too quickly against the king's forces and Northumberland had to seek refuge in Scotland. His wife and daughter-in-law are the only ladies of high rank in the play (making a telling contrast with the low-life women) and they are bitter, loveless creatures.

The Boar's Head characters

The Boar's Head is the name of the tavern in Eastcheap, a low area of London, where Falstaff and his companions regularly meet (see II.2.139-40). If the characters in the historical scenes of the play tend to be rather dull this is compensated for by the vitality and eccentricity of the play's minor comic characters. They are carefully individualised, usually by means of oddities in their appearance or speech.

Hostess Quickly, whose name in Elizabethan pronunciation has a lewd meaning, is made easily recognisable and extremely funny, by her continual misuse of words. She is coarse and common but wishes to appear to be from a higher social rank by using impressive-sounding words:

> Murder! Murder! Ah, thou honeysuckle villain, wilt thou kill God's officers and the King's? Ah, thou honeyseed rogue! Thou art a honeyseed, a man-queller – and a woman-queller.
>
> (II.1.48-51)

Here she tries to use the pretentious word 'homicide' but gets it comically wrong. The humour lies in the fact that her very efforts not to seem vulgar make her vulgarity, particularly her interest in the functions of the male body, more obvious. She is easily preyed on by Falstaff, who, being a knight, can offer her a rise in her social status by promising to marry her (II.1.96-100). Such is her vitality and warmth, in a play which is short of both, that she is one of the most likeable characters, and we think Falstaff's treatment of her cruel. However, Shakespeare must guard against the audience admiring his disorderly comic characters in a play which shows the merits of law and order. At the end of the play the Hostess is implicated in a murder. She and Doll Tearsheet are arrested by an officer:

> Come, I charge you both, go with me, for the man is dead that you and Pistol beat amongst you.
>
> (V.4.15-17)

Doll and Pistol are the two most foul-mouthed and argumentative characters in the play. They rarely say anything which is not abusive and quarrelsome. Doll does not provoke our laughter because she has no affectations; she does not pretend to be other than she is, a common prostitute. Her main function in the play is to provide, with Falstaff as her lover, a parody of romantic love (see II.4.211–16), just as the vain boaster, Pistol, provides a parody of heroism. (We have neither true love nor heroism in Part 2 although they are evident in Part 1 of *Henry IV*.)

Pistol pretends to be the exact opposite of what he really is. By joining together what he believes to be impressive scraps from popular old plays he tries to appear fearless and manly, but behind the fiery words he is a coward. Like the Hostess he is individualised by his eccentric manner of speech. He alone in the comic scenes speaks in verse rather than prose, which, as he prefers sound to sense, isolates him and makes him almost impossible to understand or communicate with:

Fear we broadsides? No let the fiend give fire!
Give me some sack. And, sweetheart, lie thou there!
Come we to full points here? And are etceteras nothings?

(II.4.177–9)

He uses words like bullets, firing them out in short, sharp bursts.

The Gloucestershire characters

There are three other comic scenes in the play and these take place at the home of Justice Shallow in Gloucestershire. Here Falstaff recruits soldiers for the campaign against the rebels, returning later to abuse Shallow's hospitality and secure money from him. The addition of these country scenes gives us the whole range of English society, from top to bottom and from town to countryside. We see how war, a game played by English nobles, affects the ordinary poor Englishman. The poorer he is the worse he is affected, as Bullcalf and Mouldy are able to bribe their way to safety (III.2.237–8). We can also see how the generous country life contrasts with that of the city and the court.

The most impressive of the Gloucestershire characters is Justice Shallow. Like the other comic characters he is limited, dominated by a single obsession (which Elizabethans called a 'humour'), and he has a comic physical oddity, extreme thinness. His obsession is with his past, which he romanticises, pretending that he had been a lusty, adventurous youth (III.2.16–23). Apart from this eccentricity, which makes him an easy prey for Falstaff, who is a friend from his youth, he runs his house, his farm and his law court with apparent efficiency, although he comically mixes all three together. It is possible to see him as a deliberate contrast to the Lord Chief Justice, one a bad and the other a good justice. His servant Davy tries to influence Shallow's judgment (V.1.33–47) but it is not clear whether he succeeds or not. If not corrupt, Shallow is certainly naive and self-deceiving, but these are follies, not crimes, and hospitable Shallow remains one of the most attractive characters in the play. His speeches at times have dignity and common sense which compare well with the mean-spirited and pretentious words of Falstaff and his crew. We see this when he cuts short Pistol's absurd language with the words:

> Give me pardon, sir. If, sir, you come with news from the court, I take it there's but two ways, either to utter them or conceal them. I am, sir, under the King, in some authority.

> (V.3.109–12)

The word 'shallow' does not adequately sum up his character, just as his fellow-justice Silence does not fulfil the expectations of his name. In Act V Scene 3 he becomes noisily merry, singing popular drinking songs in a comic reversal of his earlier meekness.

Bullcalf and Feeble also comically belie their names. Bullcalf is a coward while Feeble is given the most manly speech in the play:

> a man can die but once; we owe God a death. I'll ne'er bear a base mind. An't be my destiny, so; an't be not, so. No man's too good to serve's prince.

> (III.2.228–31)

Our confidence in Falstaff's judgment of character must be shaken when he says of Feeble:

> And for a retreat, how swiftly will this Feeble the woman's tailor run off!

> (III.2.260–1)

This is typical of the way in which Shakespeare uses a minor character to reveal a flaw in a major character. The cynical Falstaff has too narrow a view of life to allow for the bravery of Feeble or to value the hospitality of Shallow.

The language of the play

Shakespeare's language in this play had to be flexible as there is so much variety among people and places, There is a basic division between verse and prose, usually according to whether the scenes are historical or comical, verse being a more suitable medium for high and grave matters and prose for everyday, low-life scenes. The type of verse used is normally blank verse, a term applied to lines of ten alternately stressed syllables which do not rhyme:

> I pray/you take/me up,/and bear/me hence.

> (IV.4.131)

This line consists of five feet (metrical units) of two syllables each, the first unstressed and the second stressed. This basic metrical pattern is often varied by Shakespeare, and when he does so we recognise a change in the rhythm, which attracts our attention. The dramatic effect of this line, 'I know/thee not/old man./Fall to/thy prayers.' (V.5.50) is caused partly because metrical irregularity gives a special emphasis to the word 'Fall' and also to 'old' (a key word in the play); 'prayers' also receives extra emphasis because it comes after two unstressed words. It is not only what Henry V says here but the way he says it that matters.

Another variation in the verse is to use rhyme, but this is infrequent in *2 Henry IV*, though not in Shakespeare's early plays. It is used most often by Henry IV, who is the most formal speaker in the play. A number of his speeches end in a rhyming couplet and he even uses rhyme in the middle of a speech (II.1.12–13). Normally rhyme is only used for the last two lines of a scene to give a sense of finality. Verse is a sign of high rank or education, or an imitation of these. Its use in *2 Henry IV*, except by Pistol, denotes matters of high seriousness. It is more formal and rhetorical than common speech and uses more figures of speech. It lends itself to declamation, or speechifying, of which there is much in this play.

One disadvantage of the way verse is used in *2 Henry IV* is that it tends to raise all the characters to the same level of emotional intensity so that their personalities are not revealed in their manner of speech. It also makes the historical scenes slow moving, as the tendency in verse is to develop an idea in a leisurely way, often introducing extended comparison (see Lord Bardolph's speech at I.3.36–62). Because there is an artificial element in blank verse, its use can reflect badly on the speaker, who may appear more concerned with the form of his speech than its content. Shakespeare was suspicious of highly figurative language used for its own sake. Compare Lord Bardolph's speech already referred to with the economical, practical and dramatic use of verse by Henry V in his speech rejecting Falstaff (V.5.50–73). Dishonest characters in Shakespeare often hide behind the formal rhetoric of verse, and use it to conceal rather than communicate thought. The use of verse together with rhyme gives a false ring to Prince John's words after he has tricked the rebels:

> Strike up our drums, pursue the scattered stray;
> God, and not we, hath safely fought today.
> Some guard these traitors to the block of death,
> Treason's true bed and yielder-up of breath.

> (IV.2.120–3)

Choice of verse can also be a guide to character. Prince John is too stiff and self-conscious to change to prose in the presence of Falstaff (IV.3) but the Lord Chief Justice and Prince Henry, who can use prose when with the fat knight, as a result appear neither stiff nor self-conscious (I.2, II.4).

Prose is a more natural medium. It is more flexible and vigorous, being uncontrolled by any rules about metre, syllable-count or rhyme. It lends itself to spontaneous expression in informal situations when the dignity added by using blank verse would be out of place. It is therefore suited to the comic low-life scenes of this play. In these scenes the language is colloquial and often vulgar, but can be as expressive as verse and as rhetorically constructed. Notice, for example, the logical progression, repetition and balance of Falstaff's speech praising drink (IV.3.95–122). However, whereas the use of verse gives the impression of careful deliberation over choice of words, the use of prose gives the impression of relaxed spontaneity, of a man speaking without restraint. For this reason prose is particularly suitable for ranting and heated argument:

> Nut-hook, nut-hook, you lie! Come on, I'll tell thee what, thou damned tripe-visaged rascal, an the child I go with do miscarry, thou wert better thou hadst struck thy mother, thou paper-faced villain.
>
> (V.4.7–10).

The prose in *2 Henry IV*, such as this spoken by Doll Tearsheet, is so close to the colloquial language of Shakespeare's day that it can be hard to understand.

The high value which was placed on literature in Shakespeare's age was due to a belief in the power of language to persuade and improve men's minds. This sense of the power of words runs through *2 Henry IV*. Little happens in the play but there is a great deal of talking, particularly of argument and persuasion. The crucial scenes of the play are *verbal* climaxes: Prince John persuading the rebels to disband their army, the Lord Chief Justice persuading Henry V of his integrity, Lady Percy persuading Northumberland not to go to war. The most striking example of the power of words, however, is when Prince Henry is able to reverse, in the space of fifty lines, his father's settled opinion of his character, because of his 'Pleading so wisely' (IV.5.180).

Part 4

Hints for study

A PLAY NEEDS A different approach to study from that used for a novel or a poem. This is because a play is not designed for reading in a classroom but for live performance on a stage. To understand the way in which a play works you must try to think in terms of the way in which the speeches and scenes should be presented on a stage.

In Act V Scene 5, a stage direction tells us that 'the King and his train pass over the stage' and that 'Trumpets sound'. As no words are given to the characters who walk across the stage and as we cannot hear the trumpet, it is very easy for you, the reader of the play, to ignore this moment. For the Elizabethan audience, however, this is the high point in the play. It is the formal coronation procession. The trumpets raise the audience's expectations and they are dazzled by the magnificence of the king's coronation robes, which confirm his elevation to supreme majesty. To read the play as a novel is to miss this crucial piece of action. The stage direction continues, 'After them enter Falstaff, Shallow, Pistol, Bardolph, and the page'. The effect of their appearance is lost if you cannot imagine the contrast between their 'poor show' (line 13), 'stained with travel' (line 24), and the glorious procession which has just left the stage. This impact is pure theatre, managed without words, but it tells as effectively as words can why the new king must turn away his old friend.

To avoid reading a play as a novel the following hints may be useful:

(*i*) Make a note of which characters are on stage, because you can assume that the presence of each character serves some purpose.

(*ii*) Consider how they might contribute even if they are not speaking. For example, in Act II Scene 4 how will the disguised Prince Henry and Poins react when Falstaff, ignorant of their presence, insults them? To an audience the main thing happening on the stage at this time is their silent reaction.

(*iii*) Take note of visual effects indicated in the play but easily overlooked when reading. Costume, props and set are vital elements. Consider, for example, the visual impression which Falstaff's first entrance must make. He is extremely fat; he is limping and perhaps has a bandage around his foot; he is attended by a page who carries his sword and shield as if he were a great warrior. Disorder and vanity are thus established before a word has been spoken.

(*iv*) Directors and actors decide on the tone of voice which should be used for each speech. When you read a play *you* must decide on the correct tone for yourself. This can be a crucial matter in a play such as *2 Henry IV* because it is not easy to work out whether a character should be presented sympathetically or critically. How, for example, should Henry V speak the line, 'I know thee not, old man. Fall to thy prayers' (V.5.50)? It could be said gently, with a sense of loss, or coldly and distantly, or it could be said bitterly, harshly or even angrily. The choice of tone depends on your opinion of Henry in the rest of the play.

Think of a scene from the play in relationship with other scenes. The visual impression of a scene lingers on, but this is less true of verbal effects, therefore you have to make an effort to appreciate the contrast which the dramatist is making between different scenes. This is particularly important. The whole point of *2 Henry IV* depends upon contrasts, order and disorder, age and youth, authority and lawlessness, appearance and reality, and these are all brought out by careful juxtaposition (placing next to each other) of contrasting scenes.

An example of Shakespeare's conscious striving for contrastive effect can be seen by comparing the end of Act III Scene 1 and the beginning of the following scene with the end of Act IV Scene 5 and the beginning of the following scene. In both cases we move from a scene at court to Justice Shallow's house, from a mood of deep depression to a mood of light-hearted geniality. King Henry's words and the words of Shallow which follow them are almost the same in both cases:

(*i*) HENRY IV: We would, dear lords, unto the Holy Land . . .
SHALLOW: Come on, come on, come on! Give me your hand sir, give me your hand sir!
(*ii*) HENRY IV: Which vainly I supposed the Holy Land . . . In that Jerusalem shall Harry die . . .
SHALLOW: By cock and pie, sir, you shall not away tonight.

Clearly Shakespeare wants Shallow and King Henry to reflect each other. The latter is crippled by age and worry, the former shakes off old age and is buoyant. Make a note of which scenes are next to which and try to work out why they are placed together. A particularly good exercise is to explain the inclusion of Act V Scene 4, which is the only comic scene to follow a comic scene. It does not develop the plot or develop a character; what is its function? Is it merely to give time for Falstaff to travel from Gloucestershire to London, or is it to provide a contrast?

Make a note of the key images, ones which reappear throughout the play, and see how they form a coherent theme, as do those concerned with age and disease discussed above (pp. 44–6). For example, note all the references to death and how these draw together the major characters in the play, who have contrasting attitudes towards it. Falstaff is afraid of death (II.4.229–30); Shallow is undisturbed by it (III.2.32–51); Northumberland is driven half crazy by his son's death (note the 'death' references throughout I.1); Feeble is stoic: 'we owe God a death' (III.2.228); for Henry IV death is peace, the end of care, and for Prince Henry it is succession to an 'imperial crown' (IV.5.42). Try tracing other key words through the play and try to determine how their usage reflects on character. Images of disorder influence the way you react to the play and so, too, do those which come from drinking, eating, clothing, gardening, and money. Can you see any difference between the 'tavern' attitude to money (I.2.238–40 and 249–51) and the 'court' attitude to money (IV.5.67–73)?

Essay titles for plays often involve questions on character so it is essential that you should be aware of the ways in which a dramatist establishes a character:

(*i*) By what a character says and when he says it. In a novel the author can intrude into his story and tell us what a character is like or what he is thinking; the author of a play cannot walk on to the stage and guide our response. Notice also to whom the character is speaking as he might disguise his true self in front of certain people. He is most likely to be telling the truth when he is alone (for example, I.2.246–51).

(*ii*) By how a character acts, including both the choice he makes, such as Prince Henry's taking his father's crown, and the way he acts, whether he takes the crown sadly or furtively.

(*iii*) By what other characters say about him, particularly behind his back. Our attitude to a character is conditioned by the opinion others have of him and this is particularly true in *2 Henry IV* which contains a good deal of such opinion. Falstaff is very fond of reducing people to character sketches (see III.2.291–321 and V.1.56–71). Such opinions must be measured against what characters say and do. Prince Henry, for example, is difficult to pin down. Not only do characters have different opinions about him (see IV.4.54–78) but there are gaps between his words and his deeds and his private intentions.

Often in Shakespeare major characters change in response to their experiences during a play and you should be sensitive to any such developments. Prince Henry has only three hundred words to speak, so any gradual change is not possible. However, Shakespeare did not want a sudden, unconvincing transformation from bad to good so he hints that his reputation for being bad is undeserved. In this way he gives us the impression of change, Henry moving from tavern to throne, without there being a change. Is this true, or does Prince Henry change after seeing Falstaff's debauchery (II.4) and after his father's death? To help you to make up your mind, you should list all the scenes in which he appears and in which he is spoken of, and read them to see if there is a sign of change, for example in his choice of language. Apply the same method to Falstaff and ask yourself if he becomes worse as the play progresses, more vain of his reputation, less able to laugh at himself, more corrupt and disorderly.

Another way in which a play differs from other forms of literature is that we, the audience, often have more information than those participating in the action. If the characters knew what we know they would act differently. Seeing them heading for disaster we feel superior to and yet sorry for them, we feel helpless and we feel excited, awaiting the inevitable discovery that the character will make of what we already know. In a word we feel *involved*, and this is the dramatist's intention. We know about the rejection of Falstaff, for example, long before Falstaff does. It is hinted at in Act II Scenes 2 and 4, but Falstaff remains ignorant of his abandonment by the prince, and, ironically, becomes more confident of his friendship. The dramatic climax of the play comes when Falstaff is at his highest point of ignorance: 'my royal Hal . . . my sweet boy' (V.5.41–4), and the audience is at its highest point of certainty about the inevitability of the rejection. The gap between what we know and what he knows is so immense that a great tension is built up as well as a great sense of pity that Falstaff has been placed at such a disadvantage.

Writing an essay

Knowing how to write an essay is as vital as knowing the text. If you know the text well it is sensible to know also the best way to tackle an essay question. Here are a few hints:

(*i*) A question demands a reply which answers that question. If you are asked the time of day you do not describe the workings of a clock. If you are asked why Falstaff is provided with a page you do not discuss his relationship with Justice Shallow. Always be relevant and make it clear that you are being relevant from start to finish of your essay. Begin your essay 'There are four main reasons why Falstaff is provided with a page' rather than 'London in the time of Shakespeare had a population of . . . .'

(ii) Avoid repetition; even a summary in the final paragraph is a waste of time and space. The way to avoid repetition is to follow an essay plan, so that you cover a new point in each paragraph.

(iii) Illustrate every point that you make with a relevant quotation from or close reference to the text. It is not sufficient to state an idea, such as, 'The page reflects Falstaff's vanity', you must support this with evidence, a quotation or a reference. However, you must not leave a quotation for an examiner to puzzle over. Explain in what way your quotation justifies the point that you have made. For example, the line,

Give me my rapier, boy

(II.4.196)

suggests that the page holds Falstaff's sword at all times (as in Act I Scene 2), which makes Falstaff appear vain of his social status, having his own servant, and vain of his knighthood, having that servant exhibit his sword.

Specimen essay

Discuss the Induction to *2 Henry IV* and consider its relationship with the rest of the play

The Induction is the first speech of the play. It has four main functions, first to introduce the play, second to relate it with Part 1 of *Henry IV*, third to establish the mood of the play and fourth to present key ideas which will be developed in the rest of the play. The Induction is spoken by an allegorical figure called Rumour. The first half of the Induction explains what this figure represents and the second half explains his immediate purpose at the scene of the play. Rumour's first function is to give a specific introduction to the first scene of the play. Shakespeare had to inform us that King Henry IV had won and Hotspur had lost the battle of Shrewsbury. Otherwise we would miss the irony of the 'smooth comforts false' (Induction, line 40) which Rumour gives to Hotspur's father, the Earl of Northumberland, who is told that his dead son is alive. Rumour also gives a more general introduction to the play, as it states that its influence is universal (lines 2–4), and we will see later in the essay that it presides over the entire action of the play.

Its second function is to remind the audience of the events leading up to the start of the play, which take place in Part 1 of *Henry IV*. The climax of that play is the battle of Shrewsbury, which is brought into prominence in this opening speech because it leads into Act I Scene 1 and places the play in the middle of a period of civil unrest. The

Induction's third function is to establish the dominant mood of the play. Rumour appears at the most influential point in the play. His costume is strange, it is 'painted full of tongues', he speaks directly at the audience in a loud voice (line 2) and his opening words are a command to listen: 'Open your ears'. All these combine to make his appearance striking and memorable. For this reason what he says creates a mood which influences our response to and our expectations of the rest of the play. The mood established by the Induction is unpleasant and disturbing. What Rumour does is not slight but highly damaging. It 'wounds the world' (line 10) with lies which are 'worse than true wrongs' (line 40). The character of Rumour is also unpleasant. He claims power over the audience, whom he addresses as 'my household' (line 22), and he is scornful of our inability to resist the appeal of rumours:

> which of you will stop
> The vent of hearing when loud Rumour speaks?
>
> (lines 1–2)

His style of speaking is inflated and pompous and his claim that we are in his power establishes a sense of discomfort which will continue through the play, which is full of discomfiting characters and scenes.

This brings us the Induction's fourth function, which is to introduce themes which the rest of the play will develop. The Induction has a direct relationship with the first scene of the play, as he is standing before the Earl of Northumberland's house where the scene will take place (lines 35–7). In this scene we are shown the damaging effect of false rumour on Northumberland, whose hopes are raised by the report that his son is alive and has won a battle. When he hears the truth, that Hotspur is, in fact, dead and the battle lost, he is driven crazy with grief. It is not the death so much as the raised hopes which disorder his mind. He says in anguish,

> And he doth sin that doth belie the dead,
> Not he which says the dead is not alive.
>
> (I.1.98–9)

The confusion, uncertainty and wild behaviour which characterise this opening scene all stem 'From Rumour's tongues' (Induction, line 39).

The Induction also has a bearing on the play as a whole. *2 Henry IV* is a play in which words cannot be trusted and in which hopes and expectations are mocked. Prince Henry, for example, suffers from a false reputation for wildness which sours his relationship with his father and devalues him in the eyes of the world. The general expectation is that he will be a lawless king, but all who think so are misled, perhaps deliberately by the prince, who increases the rumours by mixing with Falstaff but plans to 'mock the expectation of the world' (V.2.126).

Falstaff himself is the victim of the misleading opinions about Prince Henry. When Pistol announces that the prince has become the king he asks; 'What, I do bring good news?' (V.3.126). Falstaff thinks so, but like Rumour's news it proves to be 'smooth comforts false' (Induction, line 40). Ironically the accession marks the end not the beginning of Falstaff's fortunes. Falstaff is distinctly linked with the figure of Rumour, as he says of himself, 'I have a whole school of tongues in this belly of mine' (IV.3.18), and he also admits, 'how subject we old men are to this vice of lying' (III.2.292–3). Its 'tongues' and its deceiving nature are Rumour's main characteristics. Sir John Colevile believes the false rumour of Falstaff's military reputation and it costs him his life. Similarly the Archbishop of York believes the false oath of Prince John and forfeits his life. Early in the play the archbishop had wondered, 'What trust is in these times?' (I.3.100). Both the Induction and the play which follows it demonstrate that there is none.

The above specimen essay is about one thousand words long. It is based on the following essay plan:

  (*i*) Introduction: what the Induction is, who speaks it
      Its main functions
      First function: introduces the play.
  (*ii*) Second function: links with Part 1 of *Henry IV*, battle of Shrewsbury
      Importance of place at beginning of the play
      Third function: establishes mood
      Rumour: how it is made memorable
      Nature of mood; nature of Rumour's character.
  (*iii*) Fourth function: to introduce themes developed later
      Relationship with I.1
      The effect of Rumour on Northumberland.
  (*iv*) Relationship with the rest of the play
      Expectation mocked: Prince Henry
      False hopes: Falstaff
      Falstaff as Rumour: example Colevile
      The rebels

In examinations you are often short of time so you should not try to include all the points on the topic that you may have thought of, but only the most useful ones. For example an entire section on the rhetoric and figures of speech in the Induction was left out because it took up more space than it was worth for the number of points it produced. In the same way you have to select examples to illustrate the points you do choose to make. Do not be tempted to include all the examples of a point that you can think of just to show off your knowledge. An essay is a test of your powers of organisation as well as your knowledge of the text.

Essay questions

The following questions are arranged so that the more difficult ones come lower down the list.

(1) Give an account of the character of either (*a*) Prince Henry or (*b*) King Henry IV.

(2) Discuss whether or not Prince Henry can be considered the hero of *2 Henry IV*.

(3) 'There is neither friendship, love nor heroism in *2 Henry IV*'. Discuss.

(4) 'And how absurd is Vanity, when it attempts to fence with Justice' (J. Dover Wilson). Is this an acceptable description of the relationship between Falstaff and the Lord Chief Justice?

(5) 'The "low" episodes echo their aristocratic counterparts' (Traversi). Discuss the relationship between the comic and historical scenes of *2 Henry IV* in the light of this statement.

(6) 'The shadow of age and impotence lies heavily over the action' (Traversi). Discuss this comment on *2 Henry IV*.

(7) 'Whatever might have been Shakespeare's original intention, the central figure is neither the old king nor the lean prince but the fat knight' (Sen Gupta). Consider the arguments for and against Falstaff's being viewed as the central character in *2 Henry IV*.

(8) 'A man of such pre-eminent abilities that he had a profound contempt for those around him' (Coleridge). Discuss this view of Falstaff's character in *2 Henry IV*.

(9) What influence does the deposition and murder of King Richard II have on the plot and the characters in *2 Henry IV*?

(10) Discuss whether the rejection of Falstaff is presented as a moral act or as an act of political expediency.

Part 5

Suggestions for further reading

The text

The text used throughout these notes is in the New Penguin Shakespeare series:

SHAKESPEARE: *Henry IV, Part 2,* edited by P. Davison, Penguin Books, Harmondsworth, 1977.

Another recommended edition, with fuller annotation, is in the New Arden Shakespeare series:

SHAKESPEARE: *The Second Part of King Henry IV,* edited by A. R. Humphreys, Methuen, London, 1966.

Other works by Shakespeare

Shakespeare's works have been collected in many editions. Two useful editions are:

SHAKESPEARE: *The Complete Works,* edited by P. Alexander, Collins, London and Glasgow, 1951. A reliable unannotated text.

SHAKESPEARE: *The Riverside Shakespeare*, edited by G. Blakemore Evans, Houghton Mifflin, Boston, 1974. An annotated complete works with useful prefatory essays and bibliography.

General works on Shakespeare

CAMPBELL, O. J. AND QUINN, E. G.: *A Shakespeare Encyclopaedia*, Methuen, London, 1966.

HALLIDAY, F. E.: *A Shakespeare Companion*, Penguin Books, Harmondsworth, 1964.

These are both useful reference works with entries on the works, stage history, critics and general background. They are arranged under alphabetical headings.

LLOYD EVANS, G. AND LLOYD EVANS, B.: *Everyman's Companion to Shakespeare*, J. M. Dent, London, 1978.

QUENNEL, P. AND JOHNSON, H.: *Who's Who in Shakespeare*, Weidenfeld and Nicolson, London, 1973.

The Lloyd Evans volume contains a glossary and an explanation of terms used; it has sections on biography, stage history and plot summaries. The Quennel volume is most useful for its illustrations. Both can be read continuously rather than simply used for reference purposes.

ONIONS, C. T.: *A Shakespeare Glossary*, revised edition, Oxford University Press, Oxford, 1963. The standard glossary for Shakespeare.

MUIR, K. AND SCHOENBAUM, S.: *A New Companion to Shakespeare Studies*, Cambridge University Press, Cambridge, 1971.

WELLS, S.: *Shakespeare: Select Bibliographical Guides*, Oxford University Press, London, 1973.

These are two collections of essays on various aspects of Shakespeare, and both are aimed at more advanced students. The Muir and Schoenbaum volume gathers together eighteen articles. The Wells volume is a very valuable guide to each play, with reviews of criticism and full suggestions for further reading.

Biography

SCHOENBAUM, S.: *William Shakespeare: A Documentary Life*, Clarendon Press, Oxford, 1975. The best work on Shakespeare's life.

Criticism

CAMPBELL, L. B.: *Shakespeare's 'Histories': Mirrors of Elizabethan Policy*, Huntington Library, San Marino, California, 1947.

TILLYARD, E. M. W.: *Shakespeare's History Plays*, Chatto and Windus, London, 1944.

Both of these critics – the most influential critics of the century who have written on the history plays – emphasise the necessity of placing the history plays in their period, rather than treating them as products of Shakespeare's individual genius. Miss Campbell sets out to demonstrate that Shakespeare shares the attitude towards history of his contemporaries. Her work is still the best account of what these attitudes are. Tillyard argues that Shakespeare was an orthodox thinker, who accepted the common ideas of his time. His book gives an interesting and well-argued account of the received ideas with which Shakespeare works.

REESE, M. M.: *The Cease of Majesty*, Edward Arnold, London, 1961. This author also attempts to place the history plays in context, to establish literary and dramatic precedents.

Critics of the history plays reacted against Tillyard and Campbell because they made both Shakespeare and his plays appear limited in scope. These later critics are more stimulating to read, as a general rule, because they base their arguments on the plays rather than on external sources which relate to the plays:

KNIGHTS, L. C.: *Shakespeare: the Histories*, Longman, London, 1962. This is an attempt to fit the history plays into an overall pattern of meaning.

RIBNER, I.: *The English History Play in the Age of Shakespeare*, Princeton University Press, Princeton, 1957. This critic sets out to demonstrate that Elizabethan attitudes to history were far more varied than Tillyard maintained.

ORNSTEIN, R.: *A Kingdom for a Stage*, Harvard University Press, Cambridge, Massachusetts, 1972. A general work on the history plays which treats them as drama rather than treatises.

MORGANN, M.: *Essay on the Dramatic Character of Sir John Falstaff*, London, 1777, in *Shakespearian Criticism*, edited by D. A. Fineman, Oxford University Press, Oxford, 1972.

BRADLEY, A. C.: 'The Rejection of Falstaff', in *Oxford Lectures on Poetry*, Macmillan, London, 1909. Two famous defences of the fat knight written some time ago, but still stimulating.

WILSON, J. DOVER:*The Fortunes of Falstaff*, Cambridge University Press, Cambridge, 1943. Dover Wilson sees Prince Henry as the hero in a morality play who is totally admirable.

BARBER, C. L.: 'Rule and Misrule in *Henry IV*', in *Shakespeare's Festive Comedy*, Princeton University Press, Princeton, N. J., 1959. A generous account of Falstaff as the holiday spirit, or Lord of Misrule, and an excellent general work on Shakespeare's comedy.

JENKINS, H.: *The Structural Problem in Shakespeare's Henry the Fourth*, Methuen, London, 1956. The best study of the relationships between Parts 1 and 2.

CHARLTON, H. B.: *Shakespearean Comedy*, Methuen, London, 1938. A useful discussion of the relationship between the comical and the historical scenes in *Henry IV*.

There are a number of good collections of essays, which gather together the best articles on *Henry IV*:

NICOLL, A., (ED.): *Shakespeare Survey 6*, Cambridge University Press, Cambridge, 1953.

MUIR, K. (ED.): *Shakespeare Survey 30*, Cambridge University Press, Cambridge, 1977.

HUNTER, G. K.,(ED.): *Shakespeare: King Henry IV Parts 1 and 2*, Macmillan Casebooks, London, 1970.

WAITH, E., (ED.): *Shakespeare: The Histories*, Prentice-Hall Inc., Englewood Cliffs, N. J., 1965.

YOUNG, D. P., (ED.): *Twentieth Century Interpretations of Henry IV, Part Two*, Prentice-Hall Inc., Englewood Cliffs, N. J., 1968.

The two standard studies of Shakespeare's imagery have a few remarks to make on *2 Henry IV*:

CLEMEN, W.: *The Development of Shakespeare's Imagery,* second edition, Methuen, London, 1977.

SPURGEON, C.: *Shakespeare's Imagery and What It Tells Us*, Cambridge University Press, London, 1935.

TRAVERSI, D.: 'Henry the Fourth, Part II', in *Shakespeare from 'Richard II' to 'Henry V'*, Hollis and Carter, London, 1958. This contains useful remarks on the imagery.

DANBY, J. F.: 'Henry IV, Parts 1 and 2', in *Shakespeare's Doctrine of Nature*, Faber and Faber, London, 1949. This study is influenced by the play's sombre imagery, and interprets it as a complex and ironic attack on a corrupt society.

Sources, stage and background

BULLOUGH, G.: *Narrative and Dramatic Sources of Shakespeare*, volume IV, Routledge & Kegan Paul, London, 1962.

MUIR, K.: *The Sources of Shakespeare's Plays*, Methuen, London, 1977. This discusses the use made of the sources.

BROWN, J. R.: *Shakespeare's Plays in Performance*, Penguin Shakespeare Library, Harmondsworth, 1969. This gives accounts of the play in performance.

SPRAGUE, A. C.: *Shakespeare's Histories: Plays for the Stage*, The Society for Theatre Research, London, 1964. This also gives accounts of the play in performance.

GURR, A.: *The Shakespearean Stage, 1574–1642*, Cambridge University Press, Cambridge, 1970. A good account of Shakespeare's stage.

NAGLER, A. M.: *Shakespeare's Stage*, Yale University Press, New Haven, Conn., 1958. Another good account of Shakespeare's stage.

TILLYARD, E. M. W.: *The Elizabethan World Picture*, Chatto and Windus, London, 1943. This gives a useful account of the orthodox view of the world in Shakespeare's time.

The author of these notes

MICHAEL JARDINE was educated at the University of Newcastle upon Tyne and the Shakespeare Institute of the University of Birmingham. He was a Lecturer in English Literature at Ahmadu Bello University, Nigeria, and is now a Lecturer at King Alfred's College of Higher Education, Winchester. He is writing a book on the role of the professional writer in the period from 1588 to 1624.